A NOTE FROM THE PUBLISHERS

As you enter the *Gates of Wisdom*, we hope you are able to become inspired by Rabbi Yehonatan Eybeshitz's life stories.

When we first found *The Wise Jew*, a small book written in Hebrew, we knew right away it needed to be translated into English and published for the world to read.

As you will read in the Introduction by Rabbi Barber, he, too, was inspired by the words written by Rabbi Menachem Mendel Gerlitz, and the small book *The Wise Jew* became *Gates of Wisdom*.

All the illustrations, adornments, pictures, and some of the quotes originated from *The Wise Jew*. We are including them in our new book with permission from Rabbi Gerlitz.

Am Yisrael Chai
Richie & Julie Gerber
February 2024

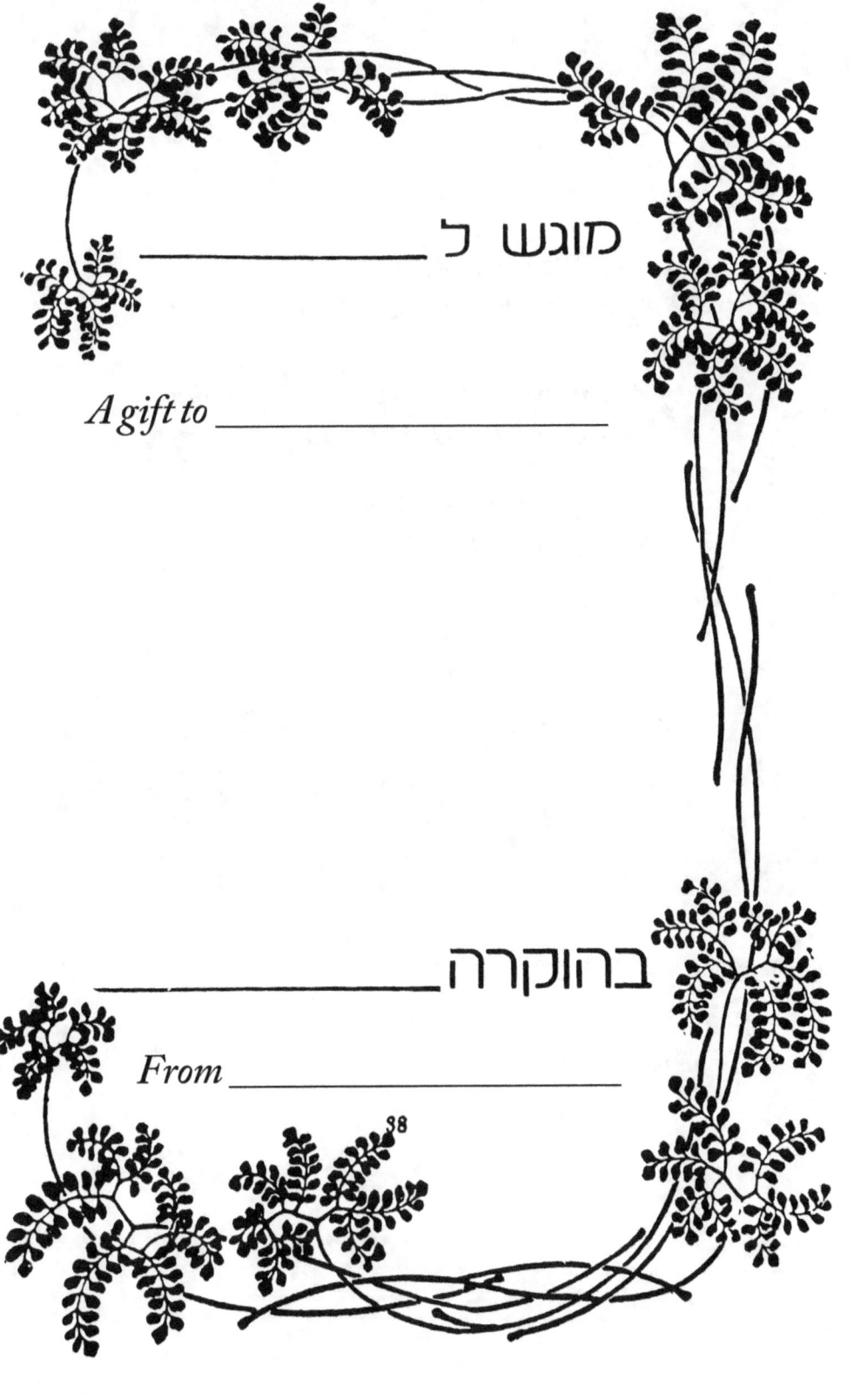

מוגש ל _____

A gift to _____

בהוקרה_____

From _____

38

Other Books in the
Rabbi Yehonatan Eybeshitz Wisdom Series

Pearls of Wisdom from Rabbi Yehonatan Eybeshitz:
Torah Giant, Preacher & Kabbalist

Sparks of Wisdom:
From Rabbi Yehonatan Eybeshitz

Gates of Wisdom

How Rabbi Yehonatan Eybeshitz Created "Am Yisrael Chai" & His Other Life Stories

Rabbi Yacov Barber

Gerber's Miracle Publishers

Published by:

Gerber's Miracle Publishers LLC
FORT LAUDERDALE, FL
GatesofWisdom.com

Copyright © 2024 Gerber's Miracle Publishers LLC

ISBN-13
979-8-9872698-2-4 (softcover)
979-8-9872698-3-1 (hardcover)

Copyediting by Carol Killman Rosenberg

Cover & Interior production by Gary A. Rosenberg

Cover photo: Main Gate to the Tower of David,
also known as The Citadel, Jerusalem, Israel

**A portion of the sales of this book
will be donated to Colel Chabad**

In memory of

All the Jews who lost their lives
in the barbaric massacre on October 7th, 2023 in Israel.
G-d bless their souls.

To the widows, orphans, injured, homeless, and traumatized Jews as a result of the massacre on October 7, 2023. May G-d deliver them a complete healing of body and spirit.

To all the courageous and heroic men and women in the Israel Defense Force, who consistently risk everything for the defense of Israel and the Jewish people.

To all the supporters and organizations providing aid and support to all the Jews who are in need.

To Colel Chabad with special thanks for their tireless service of feeding, housing, supplying shelter, and more. Colel Chabad is our ambassador on the front line, delivering tens of thousands of cooked meals to frightened families in shelters, as well as a leader in the Emergency Response Team.

Am Yisrael Chai

עם ישראל חי לעולמי עד

"The Jewish people will live for eternity."

~Rabbi Yehonatan Eybeshitz

Contents

Am Israel Chai—The How & The Why xvii

Foreword xxix

Introduction 1

Chapter 1. A Brief Overview of Reb Yehonatan's Life 5

Chapter 2. Reb Yehonatan's Youth 13

    A New Family Tree 13

    Bread and 13

    Can't Get Out of Bed 15

    A Cemetery *and* a Shul? 15

    Hide and Seek 16

    Majority Rules 17

    Payback 18

    The Junior Judge 21

    Greater Goes First 24

    When Father Enters 26

    One Less 26

    Ma Nishtanah 27

    The Stolen Afikomen 27

    Footsteps 29

    Sounds Fishy 29

The Missing Apples 30

Tasting the Fish 30

Take the Offspring 31

Hard or Soft Boiled 32

Mind Games 32

Chapter 3. Childhood Torah Thoughts 35

Why Wait to Ask the Question? 35

Would the Real King of Sodom Please Stand Up? 38

How Many Candles? 41

The Frogs 42

Honoring His Father 45

Man-Made Midrash 48

The Past Is Past 50

Bar Mitzvah Speech 51

The Purim Rabbi 54

Second Purim Torah 57

Third Purim Torah 58

Fourth Purim Torah 60

Queen Esther 61

One Test Too Many 61

The Insight 64

Chapter 4. Reb Yehonatan's Personality 67

Tree Top 67

For Free 67

Clothes Make the Man 67

Sleep 68

Was It Immersed?..68

Gold 70

Time 70

Easy and Hard...70

Humility...70

The Money Came Back 71

Baron Eybeshitz..74

Chapter 5. Interaction with Royalty 77

Pick an Entrance 77

A Cigar 78

Cat-and-Mouse Game 79

Where Are You Going? 83

Don't Drink Blood...84

The Rabbis Are the Guards.................................84

Chapter 6. Anti-Semitism.................................87

The Garden...87

Fire and Water 90

Good Business Deal 90

We Are One 92

Dressed Like Royalty 93

Walking Stick..96

Mishloach Manot 97

Forgive and Forget...98

To Bribe or Not to Bribe....................................99

Lack of Decorum...99

Blood Libel...100

Where There Are No Jews..102

At Your Wedding..102

Stand or Sit? That Is the Question...........................103

The Fence...104

The Table...106

You Are What You Eat..106

Drink This...108

You Win...110

Angels in Heaven...111

Look Me in the Eye...113

Greetings...115

Can't Change the Law..115

Horse or Donkey..116

Skinny Rooster...116

A Weighty Question...117

Majority Rules—Not Always...................................118

Rabbi Yehonatan Eybeshitz Writes "Am Yisrael
Chai" 45,760 Times to Save the Jews of Metz!............120

The Chosen People...125

Moshe Spoke the Truth...127

Seeking Revenge..127

Wealth Plays No Part...128

Chapter 7. Torah Learning.....................................131

The New Head of the Yeshiva..................................131

Cleaning House..133

When to Ask a Question...134

290 Questions..135

Never Forget..136

Oh, Is It Snowing?......................................136

Hiding in the Cemetery.................................136

Bathroom Reading Material.............................137

A Gentle Slap..138

Passed the Test..139

The Wagon Scholar......................................140

No Learning Is Learning................................141

Answering Questions....................................141

Open Book..142

The Truest Torah Thought...............................142

Sacrifice Substitute...................................142

Too Stiff..143

Like a Rock..144

Chapter 8. Mitzvot...................................145

A Beautiful Sukkah and Etrog...........................145

Medicine...145

No More and No Less....................................146

Tzedakah (Charity)...................................146

Charging Interest......................................147

Vilna Gaon...148

Chapter 9. Prayer....................................149

The Rest of the Day....................................149

With Tears...149

Permission to Speak....................................150

The Lengthy Prayer...150

The Mind Is Racing 151

Three Steps Back..152

Moshiach...152

Praying Aloud 153

True Humility 153

Shul Honors 155

Aleinu...156

Children versus Servants 157

Healing the Sick..157

Praying for the Sick...158

Chapter 10. Interaction with Community 159

Beloved 159

Rabbi of Metz 159

Over a Barrel of Wine 160

Lacking in Gratitude..161

A Question of Time 163

First off the Rank 163

The Shabbat Hagadol Speech 164

Porcelain Ornaments 167

The Butcher..167

Back to Front 168

The Holy Groom..168

Talk to One Another 169

What a Fool..169

A New Haggadah 169

Election of Leaders 170

Bris Milah.. 170

A Cold Donkey.. 171

Chapter 11. Conflict with Rabbi Yaakov Emden 173

Who Is Greater?... 173

Rabbis Are Peacemakers 174

Mind Your Own Business....................................... 174

Sticks and Stones.. 175

No Blood Flow 176

Hashem Is Eternal 177

No Rest... 179

The Amulet Crisis 180

Chapter 12. Final Days.. 181

The Last Stop.. 181

Carried... 182

On His Deathbed 182

The Maidservant 183

The Dream... 183

Glossary 187

Yaarot Dvash 192

Acknowledgments 195

Publisher's Acknowledgments................................. 199

Selected References.. 201

About the Author 203

Am Israel Chai—
The How & The Why

O n October 7, 2023, the world changed when Israel was viciously attacked by cowardly, murdering Hamas savages. Attack one Jew and you attack all Jews! This barbaric act of war and terror was met with a strong retaliation. We were and are living in shock, but we are not frozen in our grief.

Just over a month later, on November 14, 2023, more than 200,000 Jews gathered at the National Mall in Washington, DC, in what is known as the March for Israel.

Julie joined Rabbi Sruli Deitsch of the Chabad of Eastchester in his van with other members of the shul to participate in the March. While on the road, the rabbi shared a story about Julie's ancestor Rabbi Yehonatan Eybeshitz, which Julie said sent sparks of energy through her body. Rabbi Deitsch had told the story of how, in response to an antisemitic edict, Rabbi Yehonatan had coined the phrase *Am Yisrael Chai*. Later, the rabbi sent Julie a link to this story.

With great excitement, Julie forwarded me the rabbi's email, and I was astonished because this exact story was in our soon-to-be published book, *Gates of Wisdom*, which you now hold in your hands. Everyone on our team was amazed, as we had been working on this book for over a year but never connected the origins of the *Am Yisrael Chai* phrase and its significance in the Jewish soul to Rabbi Yehonatan Eybeshitz.

As Julie continued her journey, she heard the phrase *Am Yisrael Chai* chanted at pit stops and at the March itself as a declaration of defiance, solidarity, resilience, resistance, unity, pride, and indescribable emotions.

This became a "hold the presses!" moment for all of us working on completing this book. We stopped everything to spotlight Rabbi Yehonatan Eybeshitz's creation of *Am Yisrael Chai*. We will now take you through our research journey to get to the roots of this phrase.

Searching for the Roots of *Am Yisrael Chai*

"'Am Yisrael Chai' has become an anthem for the Jewish people . . . second only to Hatikvah."[1]

~*FORWARD*, NOVEMBER 23, 2023

Am Yisrael Chai

עם ישראל חי לעולמי עד

"The Jewish people will live for eternity."

~RABBI YEHONATAN EYBESHITZ

This is a declaration of defiance, solidarity, resilience, resistance, unity, and pride. It is a rallying cry . . . a battle cry worth taking up arms for. It is an ideal to live for and die for. We see this slogan on bumper stickers, T-shirts, necklaces, yard signs, flags, and many other items too numerous to mention here. But one

---

1. Gary Rosenblatt, "'Am Yisrael Chai' Has Become an Anthem for the Jewish People — but Where Did It Come From?" *Forward*, November 23, 2023, https://forward.com/culture/568200/am-yisrael-chai-jewish-anthem.

thing is for sure: It is the expression of the indomitable spirit of G-d's chosen people.

Where does this celebrated expression come from? The Torah? Midrash? Talmud? No, no, and no. In an exhaustive study of Jewish liturgy, there is absolutely no evidence of this phrase. So, we must dig deeper, but before our journey commences, it seems appropriate to analyze the statement *"The Jewish people will live for eternity."*

Who Are the Jewish People?

The Jewish people are the children of Israel (aka Jacob, also spelled Yisrael), whose 12 sons are the 12 tribes of Israel. The Midrash tells us that Jacob wrestled with a spiritual being that appeared human (an angel/man) throughout the night until dawn broke. When the unidentified man/angel beseeched Jacob to release him, Jacob demanded a blessing in exchange for doing so.[2] The man/angel acceded to Jacob's demand and named him "Israel," which means, "one who has struggled with G-d and man, and prevailed."

Interestingly, Jacob overcame his adversary but not without sustaining a physical injury—a dislocated hip. In remembrance of this event, the sciatic nerve of animals is considered non-kosher, and Jews are forbidden to eat that part of an animal.

The new name of Jacob—"Israel"—became the name of a country, nation, people, and the man who struggled with an angel. All Jews are said to be the children of Israel. And we all stood as one when the Torah was given to us at Mount Sinai.

---

2. Katia Bolotin, "6 Lessons from Jacob's Wrestling with the Angel," TheJewishWoman.org, accessed January 17, 2024, https://www.chabad.org/theJewishWoman/article_cdo/aid/5711152/jewish/6-Lessons-From-Jacobs-Wrestling-With-the-Angel.htm.

Am Yisrael Chai in Modern Times

The phrase *Am Yisrael Chai* became well known in modern times when Rabbi Shlomo Carlebach penned the song "Am Yisrael Chai" in 1965 for the Student Struggle to Save Soviet Jewry (SSSJ), a movement for whom he sang at many rallies. It not only became the SSSJ anthem but also was adopted for Jewish causes as a theme of resilience and perseverance.[3]

Rabbi Carlebach's song has a second verse, which comes directly from the Torah: *Od avinu chai,* which means "Our father lives."

Mosaic Magazine's article by Jewish author Philologos definitively states that "*am yisra'el hai . . .* though not occurring verbatim in the Bible or in classical rabbinic literature, does have its roots there." Philologo bases this on "our father lives" quote from the Bible and not as a stand-alone quote.[4]

Circling back to Rabbi Carlebach and his song, which is a couplet—"*am yisra'el hai . . . Od avinu chai*"—one needs to ask if this is the first time this phrase is used. The answer, of course, is no. Our journey for the origin of this phrase then took us to an unlikely place and time: The erev Shabbos, April 20, 1945, just five days following the liberation of the Bergen-Belsen concentration camp in Germany (where Anne Frank died of typhoid just months earlier) by British and Canadian forces.

Orthodox rabbi and British Army chaplain, Rabbi Leslie Hardman, was the first Jewish chaplain to enter the camp, two days after its liberation. Three days later, Rabbi Hardman led a formal Shabbos service.

---

3. Shlomo Carlebach Foundation, "Red Shlomo Carlebach Biography," accessed January 17, 2024, http://shlomocarlebachfoundation.org/about-reb-shlomo.

4. Philologos, "Where Does the Phrase "Am Yisra'el Hai" Come From?" *Mosaic,* May 12, 2016, https://mosaicmagazine.com/observation/israel-zionism/2016/05/where-does-the-phrase-am-yisrael-hai-come-from.

A few hundred Jews gathered among a sea of the dead (burying the bodies was a monumental task), crying, sobbing, and singing with joy over their liberation. The BBC recorded the service to document its occurrence (who would have guessed that a brief half-century later there would be Holocaust deniers). The Jews present knew they were being recorded and sang proudly for all the world to hear, even though they were sick, malnourished, and frail.

They sang "Hatikvah" (The Hope), the theme song for the Zionist movement, which is now the State of Israel's national anthem. Then at the end of "Hatikvah," Rabbi Hardman shouted, "Am Yisrael Chai! The children of Yisrael still Liveith!" Following the rabbi's exclamation, a woman cried, "Amen!"

We have now connected *Am Yisrael Chai* from Rabbi Shlomo Carlebach in 1965 to 1945, twenty years prior, being sung at the liberation Shabbat service in the Bergen-Belsen concentration camp.[5] However, since our path has not yet turned cold, let's continue our exploration.

Looking Further Back

A May 2016 article in *Mosiac Magazine* by Philologos informs us that the phrase *Am Yisrael Chai* was first notated more than 100 years ago in 1915. Philologos cites the ten-volume *Thesaurus of Hebrew Oriental Melodies* by famous musicologist Abraham Idelsohn. In this article, Philologos asserts that *Am Yisrael Chai* does not occur in the Bible or in classical rabbinical literature."[6]

---

5. Milad Doroudian, "Am Yisrael Chai: The Story Behind The Bergen-Belsen Recording," *Jewish Journal,* September 19, 2014, https://jewishjournal.com/culture/food/133516.

6. Philologos, "Where Does the Phrase "Am Yisra'el Hai" Come From?" *Mosaic,* May 12, 2016, https://mosaicmagazine.com/observation/israel-zionism/2016/05/where-does-the-phrase-am-yisrael-hai-come-from.

Does the origin of *Am Yisrael Chai* go only as far back as a 100-year-old book? In *The Forward*, a headline reads, *"Contrary to popular belief, the stirring song does not date back centuries"*[7] If we accept that, we have indeed reached the end of our quest. *Am Yisrael Chai* was first seen 100 years ago in a Jewish music book. Are they correct . . . or was the phrase used prior to 1915?

Researching 100 years prior, in the 1800s, we discover that there is no mention of *Am Yisrael Chai*. Not willing to give up we search for *Am Yisrael Chai*, *we went* all the way back to 1750 with no success. Apparently, *The Forward* headline had it right: *Am Yisrael Chai* does *not* go back centuries. Our search back 275 years ago leaves us empty-handed. Maybe it's time to bail out and accept that *Am Yisrael Chai* was a creation of the twentieth century—Fortunately, we know otherwise.

Amulets

Let's digress for a moment and explore the significance of amulets. Amulets in various forms have been used for millennia for a variety of purposes. People would use these pieces of parchment with special blessings and images to be protected from sickness and disease and to repel demons and the evil eye (*ayin hara*). Some amulets were intended to bless and protect women in childbirth as well as their newborns.

Some amulet parchments were divided into squares from nine to over 100 boxes in all. Hebrew letters fill the boxes, forming an acrostic with a hidden spiritual verse. Not all amulets were created equal. The inscription as well as the person writing it impacted its power. The effectiveness of the amulet rested on the righteousness of the author.

---

7. Gary Rosenblatt, "Am Yisrael Chai' Has Become an Anthem for the Jewish People — but Where Did It Come From?" *Forward*, November 23, 2023, https://forward.com/culture/568200/am-yisrael-chai-jewish-anthem

The most renowned Hebrew scholar in the Middle Ages, Maimonides, was opposed to use of amulets, but Nahmanides and the Gaon of Vilna both endorsed their use.[8]

Rabbi Yehonatan Eybeshitz—Master Amulet Maker

Besides Rabbi Yehonatan's brilliance as a Torah, Talmud, and Kabbalah genius, he was considered one of the most renowned amulet makers of his time. As mentioned, the power of the amulet rested not only on the righteousness, experience, and expertise of the maker but also on the words and symbols written on it.

Rabbi Yehonatan was a towering figure as a tzaddik, and his righteousness and experience were beyond reproach, making him the perfect candidate for master amulet maker. While he was the rabbi of Metz, France, Rabbi Yehonatan wrote amulets for expectant mothers. His success in helping these women spread throughout the city of Metz and far beyond. He gained a reputation for being a brilliant and highly respected amulet writer.

Rabbi Yehonatan Writes *Am Yisrael Chai* 45,760 Times to Save the Jews of Metz!

Miracle of miracles, wonder of wonders? We finally discover *Am Yisrael Chai* written on a piece of parchment the size of a mezuzah scroll. But even more miraculous is the fact that *Am Yisrael Chai* is written on this small two-inch by four-inch scroll 45,760 times!

Impossible!   *Incredible!*   *Unimaginable!*

Inconceivable!   *Preposterous!*

---

8. "Amulet," Jewish Virtual Library, accessed January 17, 2024, jewishvirtuallibrary.org/amulet.

And to take this even further, *Am Yisrael Chai* was written on this small parchment to protect the Jews of Metz, France, from being expelled. To get a rudimentary understanding of how this genius accomplished this task, turn to page 120 of this book for the full story.

Mission Accomplished

Our journey led us to the "who" and "why" of *Am Yisrael Chai*. The great Rabbi Yehonatan Eybeshitz spoke those words to a prince in defiance of the prince's Jew-hating edict. Rabbi Yehonatan turned his words into the first known written document of the phrase. But is this the grand finale of our story? No! It is just the beginning.

> *"The tzaddik is here with us after his passing even more than before."*
>
> ~THE ZOHAR

During his lifetime, the tzaddik was limited within a physical body. Now he has transcended those limitations.[9]

Rabbi Yehonatan Eybeshitz wrote *Am Yisrael Chai* in an amulet more than 275 years ago to successfully save Jews from a Jew-hating prince. Using his brilliance, he placed powerful words infused with prayer and intent on a small piece of parchment. Those words have transcended the limitations of time and space to become more powerful today than ever.

---

9. Tzvi Freeman, "Is It OK to Ask a Deceased Tzaddik to Pray for Me?" Chabad.org, accessed January 17, 2024, https://www.chabad.org/library/article_cdo/aid/562222/jewish/Is-It-OK-to-Ask-a-Deceased-Tzaddik-to-Pray-for-Me.htm.

For us, *Am Yisrael Chai* is a vision for the future—a light for the Jews to remember for all time:

עם ישראל חי לעולמי עד

Am Yisrael Chai Lolom Voed

"The Jewish people will live for eternity."

~Rabbi Yehonatan Eybeshitz

Richie & Julie Gerber
February 2024

Replica of the amulet created by Rabbi Yehonatan Eybeshitz *"Am Yisrael Chai"* (The Jewish People will Live for Eternity!).

The phrase is written 45,760 times in Kabbalist code.

Learn its mystical secrets on page 120!

"...וַאדֹנִי חָכָם כְּחָכְמַת מַלְאַךְ הָאֱלֹקִים
לָדַעַת אֶת כָּל אֲשֶׁר בָּאָרֶץ" (ש"ב יד, כ)

My Lord is wise, according to the wisdom of an angel
of Hashem to know all that is in the earth.

(Shmuel II 14:20)

"הַחָכְמָה תָּעֹז לֶחָכָם מֵעֲשָׂרָה
שַׁלִּיטִים אֲשֶׁר הָיוּ בָּעִיר" (קהלת ז, יט)

Wisdom affords strength to the wise more than
ten rulers who were in the city

(Kohelet 7:19)

מָרָן הַגָּאוֹן הַקָּדוֹשׁ רַבִּי יְהוֹנָתָן אִיבְּשִׁיץ זי"ע
(ת"ן – תקכ"ד)

Our master the holy genius Rabbi Yehonatan Eybeshitz—
His memory should be a blessing (1696*–1764)

*The Hebrew date is 1690, however the accepted opinion is that Reb Yehonatan was born in 1696.

FOREWORD

From *The Wise Jew*

Among the great and righteous Jews of the last few hundred years, the great Torah scholar Reb Yehonatan Eybeshitz has illuminated the Jewish world with his unique light. He has awakened within us a sense of pride that we are able to say that we are from the same nation that has produced a person of such stature.

Reb Yehonatan was blessed with a sharp, and incredible mind. His work the *Urim V'Tumim* is studied by Torah scholars who seek to plumb the depths of Torah scholarship. Reb Yehonatan was a holy and righteous person and an outstanding Kabbalist. His students would compare him to Rambam in his proficiency in the revealed areas of the Torah and to the holy Rabbi Isaac Luria (Arizal) in the hidden areas of the Torah.

Well known for his efforts on behalf of the Jewish community, Reb Yehonatan on many occasions was successful in nullifying evil decrees against the Jewish people due to his ability to finding favor in the eyes of kings and princes.

As one of the leaders of his generation, he served as a rabbi in many different prestigious communities. He introduced various decrees to enhance and strengthen the Jewish faith. His speeches and lectures had a profound impact on the Jewish people, and he was successful in guiding many Jews who had drifted from their faith to reconnect with the Torah.

Reb Yehonatan possessed many incredible qualities that at times seemed to be contradictory. On the one hand he was extremely humble, while on the other, he was a leading activist, who worked with great unwavering diligence and was always the first to be vocal when the need arose. He was a masterful Kabbalist and many great secrets were revealed to him, yet he was well versed in many different fields of knowledge.

While his very lofty soul contained within it many incredible and profound qualities, it is Reb Yehonatan's wisdom that stands out. It is this same form of wisdom that Yoseph displayed before Pharaoh in Egypt and the Daniel the Prophet demonstrated before King Nebuchadnezar.

When a Jew studies Torah with a pure heart and performs the commandments with self-sacrifice and he displays great humility and reverence, such a person becomes elevated and can therefore influence kings and princes; more important, however, Reb Yehonatan was revered by all Jews.

Rabbi Menachem Mendel Gerlitz z"l
Jerusalem

Postscript

During the writing of this book, we were informed of the untimely passing of Rabbi Menachem Mendel Gerlitz in March 2022. Here are a few words shared by his family:

As a Remembrance

The writer of our book, the Gaon and Chassid Rabbi Yitzchak Menachem Mendel Gerlitz of righteous memory, was the head and founder of the Torah organization Orayta Aderet.

He was the son of the Rav and Chassid Reb David Tzvi of righteous memory. He passed away on 3 Adar 2, 5782. He is buried on Har HaZeitim facing the Holy Temple.

This great man, scribe, and author, was a powerful and great giant of spirit and vision of action, the creator of the Torah revolution in the previous generation.

He published the manuscripts of the early scholars and the Torah scholarship of the latter scholars, and enhanced them with his clarifications and comments.

And produced superlative works that captivate the soul, including biographies of the great luminaries of Torah and Chassidut, and the chronicles of Torah Judaism and Hasidic life in the Holy Land and the Diaspora.

He benefited the populace by writing close to one hundred books in all areas of the Torah, in which he set his seal for future generations.

May His Soul Be Bound with the Eternal Light

INTRODUCTION

This is the third book in the Rabbi Yehonatan Eybeshitz series. The first is *Pearls of Wisdom,* which shares with the English-speaking world a glimpse of Reb Yehonatan's thoughts on the weekly Torah readings, the festivals, and the final redemption. I tried to be as true to his written word as possible while ensuring that English readers could understand his teachings.

The second in the series, *Sparks of Wisdom,* intends to impress upon the English-speaking audience how the teachings of a man born in 1696 are as relevant today as they were then. Hopefully, I accomplished this by not confining myself to a definitive translation of the texts cited. I also took the liberty of supplementing each thought with modern-day application.

This third book, *Gates of Wisdom,* has been a true labor of love. Initially, the intention was for me to translate *The Wise Jew* by Rabbi Menachem Mendel Gerlitz, which was written in Hebrew. In his introduction, Rabbi Gerlitz writes, "This book contains many stories of Reb Yehonatan that demonstrate his brilliant mind. These stories have been lovingly shared from one generation to the next. I hope the reader will equally enjoy these stories."

After concluding the translation of *The Wise Jew,* this book took on a life of its own. I discovered countless other stories.

Each story I encountered was like a rare diamond seen for the first time. And just when I thought I had uncovered all known stories, I was amazed to discover that was not the case. In total, I researched more than 15,000 books in which Reb Yehonatan's name is mentioned.

My hope is that you will recognize that this is more than just a book of stories. The Talmud relates how the great Rabbi Akiva[1] followed Rabbi Yehoshua[2] around to see how he conducted himself and act in kind. And this was true of other such sages of that era. In more recent times, Reb Leib Saras[3] said, "I do not go to Maggid of Mezritch [4] to learn the interpretations of the Torah. I go to him to observe his way of tying his shoelaces." When reading these stories, remember that there are life lessons to be learned from Reb Yehonatan's behavior.

Furthermore, our rabbis teach us that not only must we learn from the conduct of great rabbis, but also the conversations of Torah scholars require analysis, even when the conversation is not to issue a halachic ruling. The Hebrew word *Torah* means "instruction." It is not by chance that a large percentage of the Torah is comprised of stories, as the Torah recognizes the power of the story to influence the minds and hearts of men.

The power of the story is profoundly depicted in the following Chassidic tale:

---

1. A leading Jewish scholar and sage, a tanna (teacher) of the latter part of the first century and the beginning of the second century; a leading contributor to the *Mishnah*.

2. A leading *tanna* (teacher) of the first half-century following the destruction of the Second Temple.

3. Rabbi Leib Sarah's—Aryeh Leib the son of Sarah—(1730–1796; a Hasidic rabbi, great scholar, and a disciple of the Baal Shem Tov and the Maggid of Mezritch.

4. Reb Dov Ber Mezeritch (1704–1772); a disciple of the Baal Shem Tov.

When the great Rabbi Yisroel Baal Shem Tov[5] saw misfortune threatening the Jews, it was his custom to go into a certain part of the forest to meditate. There he would light a fire, say a special prayer, and the miracle would be accomplished and the misfortune averted.

Later when his disciple, the celebrated Maggid of Mezritch, had occasion for the same reason to intercede with heaven, he would go to the same place in the forest and say, "Master of the Universe, listen! I do not know how to light the fire, but I am still able to say the prayer." And again the miracle would be accomplished.

Still later, Rabbi Moshe-Leib of Sassov, in order to save his people once more, would go into the forest and say, "I do not know how to light the fire, I do not know the prayer, but I know the place and this must be sufficient." It *was* sufficient, and the miracle would be accomplished.

Then it fell to Rabbi Yisroel of Ruzhin to overcome misfortune. Sitting in his armchair, his head in his hands, He spoke to God: "I am unable to light the fire, and I do not know the prayer; I cannot even find the place in the forest. All I can do is to tell the story, And this must be sufficient." And it was.

We have been telling the story of the Jewish people for more than 3,000 years, transmitted from one generation to the next. My prayer is that the stories of Reb Yehonatan in *Gates of Wisdom* will be transmitted from generation to generation, and that they will continue to inspire and guide us as we draw closer to Hashem.

Rabbi Yacov Barber

---

5. Rabbi Israel Baal Shem-Tov, founder of the Chassidic Movement b. 1698 d. 1760

CHAPTER 1

A BRIEF OVERVIEW OF REB YEHONATAN'S LIFE

On the 6th of Cheshvan, 1696, in Pintshov, Poland, the home of Reb Nossan Nota and his wife, Shaindel, was filled with light. They were blessed with the birth of a son who would eventually illuminate the Jewish world with his Torah wisdom. They named him Yehonatan.

Reb Yehonatan descended from some of the greatest and holiest rabbis of all time. His father, the Gaon Reb Nossan Nota, was a descendent of the Megaleh Amukos.[6] His mother, Shaindel, was the daughter of the av bet din of Helishoi and Pintshov, Reb Yehuda Leib Tzuntz, who was a descendant of the Mahra"m Schiff.[7] In fact, Yehonatan's lineage could be traced all the way back to King David himself.

Even as a child, Yehonatan was renowned as one of the rare geniuses of his times. He served as rabbi of various communities

---

6. Rabbi Nathan Nota Spira, who lived in Poland 1585–1633. One of the great rabbis of his times. On his tombstone it is inscribed that he merited to see Eliyahu Hanavi Elijah the Prophet.

7. Rabbi Meir ben Ya'akov HaKohen Schiff 1605–1641 was a German rabbi and Talmud scholar. At the age of seventeen, he was called to the rabbinate of Fulda.

for more than fifty years. He founded and led yeshivot for most of his life. His students would become the leading rabbis and teachers of the next generation.

Yehonatan's mother passed away when he was just a young boy. When Yehonatan was eleven years old, his father was appointed as av bet din and the rosh yeshiva in the city of Eybeshitz (Morovia). The young Yehonatan attended his father's yeshivah, but tragically, a year after his appointment, Yehonatan's father passed away.

The rabbis of Eybeshitz felt that Yehonatan should relocate to the yeshivah of Rabbi Meir Eisenstadt. He took with him the surname Eybeshitz, and hence was known as Yehonatan Eybeshitz. He became a beloved student of Rabbi Meir Eisenstadt's yeshivah.

Reb Yehonatan excelled in his learning, and many sought him as a suitable husband for their daughters. In 1710, at the age of fourteen, Reb Yehonatan married Elkeli, the daughter of Rabbi Yitzchak Shapiro. After his marriage, the young couple moved to Rabbi Yitzchak's hometown of Bemusela, where Rabbi Yitzchak was the rosh yeshiva. A year later, Rabbi Yitzchak appointed Reb Yehonatan, only fifteen years old, as the rosh yeshiva.

That same year, in 1711, Reb Yehonatan relocated to the city of Prague and learned under his father-in-law's father, Rabbi Aharon Yechiel Michel Shapiro. He also studied under his father-in-law's grandfather, Rabbi Benyamin Wolf, who was the av bet din and the rabbi of the city. He also studied under the Korban Netanel.

In 1713, an epidemic broke out in Prague. Reb Yehonatan, together with his wife and small children, moved to Hamburg, where his mother-in-law's father, Rabbi Mordechai Cohen, lived. A year later, in 1714, the darshan of Prague passed away, and the rabbis of Prague requested that Reb Yehonatan accept

פֶּרֶק בְּיוֹנָי

אויף די הבעל הטורים

The Jewish Quarter in Prague

the position. In that role and beyond, his speeches electrified his audiences, and synagogues were filled whenever he spoke. There were times when he would speak for seven to eight hours!

A mere few months after being appointed as darshan, Reb Yehonatan was appointed as the rosh yeshiva of the yeshivah of Prague. During the years as rosh yeshiva, Rabbi Yehonatan's fame spread throughout the Jewish world. Questions were sent to him from great distances. His fame also spread among the gentile world. He debated many leaders of the church. As a result of his close relationship with the heads of the church, he was permitted to print the Talmud at a time when it was virtually forbidden.

Twenty-three years after being appointed the darshan of Prague, the av bet din, Rabbi Dovid Oppenheim, passed away. As a result, Reb Yehonatan was appointed av bet din. He now held three positions in Prague: the darshan, rosh yeshiva, and av bet din.

After spending twenty-eight years in Prague, Reb Yehonatan and his family moved to Metz in France. There he built a yeshivah, which flourished. In 1750, the communities of Altona, Hamburg, and Wandsbek (which had a printing house) appointed him as chief rabbi. He was keen to move to that area, as he wanted very much to print his writings, and there were no printing houses in Metz.

Soon after arriving at his new rabbinical post, Reb Yehonatan became embroiled in a dispute between himself and Rabbi Yaakov Emden that engulfed much of the Jewish world. You see, a number of years prior, a man by the name of Shabbtai Zvi had claimed to be the messiah, and many Jewish people accepted him as such, causing a rift in the Jewish world. It soon became evident, however, that Shabbtai Zvi was a fraud. The basis of the dispute was that Rabbi Emden accused Reb Yehonatan of being a secret follower of this false messiah.

בֶּחָכָם בִּיהוּדִי

רַבָּה שֶׁל פְּרָג הגה״ק רַבִּי יְחֶזְקֵאל לַנְדְאוּ בַּעַל הַ״נוֹדָע בִּיהוּדָה

The Rabbi of Prague, Rabbi Yechezkel HaLevi Landau,
author of the *Noda B'Yehuda*

As a great kabbalist, Reb Yehonatan was known to write amulets containing kabalistic writings to bless the sick.[8] During a terrible plague that was sweeping through the Jewish community, many pregnant women had come to him for a blessing. Based on false evidence from Reb Yehonatan's opposition, Rabbi Emden pointed to one of these amulets (purported to have been written by Rabbi Yehonatan) and claimed that the language used indicated that he was a secret Shabbtai Tzvi follower. Reb Yehonatan denied these claims on numerous occasions over the years. Nevertheless, the dispute lasted until 1756, when it became evident that the attacks on Reb Yehonatan had been fabricated.

During this time, Reb Yehonatan's beloved wife, Elkele, passed away in 1755. On the 21st of Elul 1764, at the age of sixty-eight, Rabbi Yehonatan returned his soul to his creator. The pair had been blessed with six sons (Reb Yehudah Leib, Reb Yitzchak, HaRav Nosson Nota, Reb Mordechai, Reb Yechiel Michel, and Reb Binyamin Zev) and three daughters (Rivkah, Hitzel, and Nisel).

Reb Yehonatan's legacy includes many seforim on all sections of the Torah. His main works on halacha are the *Urim V'Tumim on Shulchan Aruch Choshen Mishpat* and *Kreisi U'Plasi on Shulchan Aruch Yore De'ah*. He wrote a book on *Drush* (homiletics and exegesis defining and explaining the verses of the Torah) called the *Yaarot DeVash*. In total, he wrote more than ninety scholarly works.

---

8. An amulet is an object, often a charm or piece of jewelry, that is believed to possess certain powers of protection. Amulets have a long history in Jewish practice and their use was accepted by the ancient rabbis, who appeared to believe in their power. References to amulets are found throughout the Talmud, which suggests that the practice of keeping them was a common one. One Talmudic passage suggests that amulets were used by ancient rabbis to repel demons. The Talmud even states that one may carry an amulet in public on Shabbat, provided it was made by an "expert."

ABOUT THE STORIES

The stories in the following chapters offer us a small gateway into the life of one of the greatest rabbis of the last 500 years. They are loosely grouped by category, but you can skip around if you would like to get glimpses of Reb Yehonatan's brilliance from different areas and times in his life.

Some stories convey the heights of genius that Reb Yehonatan climbed. From an incredibly young age, it was evident that his mind was lightning fast, and he demonstrated an incredible ability to remember all that he had learned. His mind was truly like a computer.

To help you appreciate and marvel in the genius, many stories are supplemented with background material. Most often, the background provides just a few notes to help some readers better understand the stories. However, at times, the background may be longer than the story, but don't be put off. Read the background a few times before beginning the story and review it again after reading the story.

Some of the stories and conversations included need to be studied and reread several times to fully appreciate and fathom the mind of this genius.

בֶּחָכָם בְּיִהוּדִי

CHAPTER 2

REB YEHONATAN'S YOUTH

A New Family Tree

When Yehonatan was a little boy, his family lost their most prized possession: their family tree. Yehonatan's parents were extremely upset as the family tree showed that the family were descendants of great rabbis. Yehonatan saw how distressed his parents were and told them not to worry or be upset as he would begin a new chapter in the family history—and he would begin a new family tree. Yehonatan was a boy of his word: He grew up to become the great Reb Yehonatan Eybeshitz.

Bread and . . .

When Yehonatan was about five years old, a renowned rabbi had come to visit. The rabbi enjoyed talking to the boy and observing his brilliant mind. One day, the rabbi asked him, "Yehonatan, what did you eat for breakfast?"

Yehonatan responded, "Bread with—" Before he could finish the sentence, the rabbi picked himself up and walked out of the house.

בֶּחָכָם בְּיְהוּדִי

נִגַּשׁ הָרַב אֶל יְהוֹנָתָן וּשְׁאָלוֹ:

"בַּמֶּה?"

"בְּחֶמְאָה!" — עָנָה הַיֶּלֶד.

טָפַח הָרַב עַל שִׁכְמוֹ שֶׁל הַקָּטָן וְחִיֵּךְ חִיּוּךְ
רָחָב כְּאוֹמֵר: אָכֵן זֶה יֶלֶד בַּעַל שֵׂכֶל וּבַעַל זִכָּרוֹן
כְּאֶחָד!

About a year later, the same rabbi came back for another visit. He went over to Yehonatan asked, "With what?"

As quick as a flash, Yehonatan replied, "With butter."

The rabbi tapped him on the forehead and said, 'This boy is brilliant and possesses an incredible memory."

Can't Get Out of Bed

When Reb Yehonatan was a young boy, he once went walking with his father, and they passed by a prison. His father explained that the prisoners had to be locked up and not allowed to roam the streets because they were dangerous and the citizens of the country had to be protected.

In his innocence, Yehonatan told his father that he had a simpler solution: "Why don't the authorities simply take away their *negel vasser,* and then they won't be able to get out of bed."

A Cemetery *and* a Shul?

When Yehonatan was a little boy, his father was a rabbi in a small village that had a shul and a cemetery. There were exactly ten men—enough for a minyan.

One day, a traveler passed through and asked Yehonatan, "Why do you have a shul *and* a cemetery? If one man dies, then there's no need for the synagogue, and if no man dies, then there's no need for the cemetery."

Yehonatan answered, "We pray and hope that no men will pass away, and that is why we need the shul. The cemetery is for people who are passing through town."

Hide and Seek

The king had heard about a Jewish child called Yehonatan, who was extremely brilliant. He asked that Yehonatan be brought to the palace. The king gave strict instructions that none of his guards or ministers should direct the child to the king's chambers. Rather, they should point him in different directions to test his brilliance.

When Yehonatan arrived, he was given different directions to the king's chambers by many different people, and he was unsure where to go. So he went outside and studied the front of the palace. He then knew exactly where to go and headed that way.

The king was amazed that Yehonatan had discovered the location of his chambers, and Yehonatan explained, "I went outside, and I saw all the windows were open to let in the breeze, but one room had its windows closed and the shades drawn. I immediately knew that the king would be in that room."

As they talked, a question occurred to the king, and he asked, "Your Torah states you should follow the majority, so then shouldn't you convert to our faith, as we are far greater in number than you are?"

Yehonatan responded, "When I was looking for your chambers, I would have followed the majority if I had had any doubt. However, once I had been outside and seen the windows, I knew exactly where to go; therefore, it became irrelevant how many people said I was going the wrong way. Likewise, we, the Jewish people, saw Hashem at Mount Sinai, and we know the truth. It is irrelevant then how many people think differently than we do."

Majority Rules

Note: This story is a variation of the previous story, and while some specifics differ, Yehonatan's wisdom remains consistent.

It was common knowledge that Yehonatan was a child prodigy. Even the king was intrigued by him and wanted to meet him. The king was close friends with Yehonatan's father, the town rabbi, so he asked him to please have Yehonatan pay him a visit.

Wanting to test how smart the boy was, the king told Yehonatan's father that he was not allowed to tell his son the location of the palace; the boy would need to find it on his own. They decided that Yehonatan would arrive the next day at two o'clock in the afternoon.

The next morning, Yehonatan's father told him that the king wanted to see him but that he was not permitted to tell him the way. So Yehonatan stopped someone on the street to ask for directions. The passerby told him to make a right at the fork in the road and that path would eventually reach the palace, which it did.

The king had instructed his officers and soldiers to surround his chamber with their swords drawn to scare Yehonatan from entering, but Yehonatan feared no one but Hashem Himself. He pushed past the officers and entered the king's inner chamber. The king was astonished by the boy's boldness and asked him how he had found the palace.

Yehonatan replied that he had asked a stranger who told him to take a right at the main crossroad.

Further testing Yehonatan's intelligence, the king then asked him what he would have done if a second person had told him to go left. Yehonatan answered that, according to Jewish law, when a person isn't sure what to do, he should follow the majority. Yehonatan said he would have asked a third person and followed their directions.

The king thought he had trapped the young genius and called for the bishop to convert him. He told Yehonatan that if he followed the majority and the majority of the world was not Jewish, then Yehonatan needed to convert.

Yehonatan asked the king for permission to ask a question. When granted, he asked, "If I was standing in the palace, and I see this beautiful chamber with all its gold and silver, and in front of me, I see the king with a crown covered in diamonds and rubies on his head, and imagine if a hundred people would come into this room and tell me that this is not the king's chamber and this is not the king; rather the king's palace and the king are in another part of the city—who do you think I should believe? Should I believe what I see or what people are telling me?"

The king immediately answered, "Of course, what you see."

Yehonatan replied, "My dear king, the same is true when it comes to the Jewish faith. I have no doubts. I know for sure that there is Hashem, and I even remember who was standing next to me at Mount Sinai. In such circumstances, following the majority makes no sense at all."

The king instructed his men to fill the young boy's pockets with gold coins and to send him home, as he was concerned that this child prodigy just might convince him to convert to Judaism.

Payback

One fine morning, Yehonatan was walking to school when he was attacked and beaten by a vicious man who was an anti-Semite. Yehonatan was quite scared and began to cry. But then he calmed himself and said to his attacker, "Today is your lucky day."

בֶּחָכָם בִּיהוּדִי

"אֲנִי, לֹא הָיָה בְּאֶפְשָׁרוּתִי לְהִתְנַקֵּם בַּגּוֹי כָּרָאוּי לוֹ, שֶׁכֵּן גָּדוֹל וְחָזָק הוּא מִמֶּנִּי, לָכֵן בָּדִיתִי מִלִּבִּי אֶת הַסִּפּוּר בִּדְבַר הַ'פְּרָס', כִּי בָּרוּר הָיָה לִי, שֶׁכָּךְ יֵלֵךְ לְחַפֵּשׂ לוֹ קָרְבָּן מִבֵּין הַיְּהוּדִים הָעֲשִׁירִים, וְ'הַהוּא' כְּבָר יְשַׁלֵּם לוֹ גַּם עֲבוּרִי!..."

"Why?" asked the anti-Semite.

Yehonatan explained, "Today is a special day on the Jewish calendar. Today's rule is that, if a Jew is attacked by a non-Jew, then the Jew must give any money in his pocket to his attacker."

Yehonatan then took the few coins his mother had given him to buy a snack out of his pocket and gave it to the anti-Semite.

The anti-Semite got to thinking and came up with a plan: *Why waste my time beating up poor Jewish boys? Let me attack one of the wealthy and important Jews in the city, and then he will have to give me all his money, and I will become very wealthy.*

The anti-Semite then went into the city square and attacked a wealthy, important Jew. The wealthy Jew began screaming, and in a matter of moments, people came to his rescue. They held the attacker until the police arrived.

When the police took the criminal to the police station, they asked him, "Why did you do such a stupid thing? You attacked one of the most important and wealthiest Jews in the city in broad daylight."

The anti-Semite responded, "A Jewish boy told me that today is a special day for the Jews, and if a Jew is attacked today, he has to give all the money in his pocket to his attacker."

After some investigation, the police discovered that the young boy was none other than the rabbi's son Yehonatan. The police brought young Yehonatan to the station and asked him why he had tricked the non-Jew.

Yehonatan explained, "Earlier today, this man attacked me. I am only a child. I couldn't defend myself against him, so I quickly told him the lie that today non-Jews are rewarded for hitting a Jew. I knew he would go looking for a wealthy Jew to attack, and the wealthy Jew would make sure this attacker was brought to the police."

The Junior Judge

Yehonatan's father was the chief rabbi of Pintshov. At one time, the Jews of Pintshov were in grave danger, and it was the young Yehonatan with his brilliant mind who saved them. The story goes as follows:

A Jew owned a small spice store next to a butcher shop, which was owned by a non-Jew. Only a flimsy partition separated the two stores, so it was quite easy to see what was going on in the adjacent store.

One day, as the Jew was about to close the store, he counted all the coins he had made that day and separated them into piles. In the first pile, he placed all the gold coins; in the second pile, all the silver coins; and in the third pile, all the copper coins. He then placed all the coins in the drawer.

Meanwhile, as the Jew counted his coins, the butcher was watching from between the cracks of the partition and counted along with him. Then, the next morning, when the Jew came to open his spice store, the butcher waited outside and shouted that the Jew had stolen all his money. He said he could prove it because he knew exactly how many gold, silver, and copper coins the Jew had stolen from him, and they would surely be in the drawer where the Jew kept his coins.

The police came and counted the money, and it was the exact amount the butcher had said. They surmised that the only way the butcher could have known the exact amount of each pile was if the Jew had stolen the coins from him. The Jew was arrested and thrown into jail.

The non-Jews used this incident as an excuse to accuse all Jews of being thieves, saying that they could not be trusted. This stoked the fire of the hatred toward the Jews. Yehonatan's father gathered all the elders of the community to think of how they could prove the innocence of the Jew.

בֶּחָכָם בִּיהוּדִי

נֶאֱלַץ לְהוֹדוֹת בְּפִשְׁעוֹ לְעֵין כֹּל...

הַיְהוּדִי שֻׁחְרַר מִמַּאֲסָרוֹ, וְלַיְהוּדִים הָיְתָה
אוֹרָה וְשִׂמְחָה.

כָּךְ הִצִּיל הַיֶּלֶד הֶחָכָם, בֶּן הָרַב, אֶת יְהוּדֵי
פִּינְטְשׁוֹב מִסַּכָּנַת פְּרָעוֹת.

The next day, Yehonatan and his friends from cheder were playing during their lunch break. They decided to play a game called the butcher store and spice store. One of the boys would be the Jew who owned the spice store, and the other boy would be the butcher. Yehonatan said he would be the judge.

As they were about to present their claims to the "junior judge," one of the community leaders was walking past and heard what the boys were about to do. He stood to the side to avoid being seen.

As he watched, the boys acted out what had happened. The boy playing the butcher said that the Jew stole his money, and the boy playing the spice store owner said, "I didn't steal your money. The money is mine."

After hearing both boys, Yehonatan said, "We should place all the coins in a large bowl of boiling hot water and let us see if there are bubbles in the water."

Yehonatan explained that since the butcher touched meat all day, his hands would be covered in meat fats, and he would transfer the grease to the coins. The grease in the hot water would cause bubbles to rise. "If there are bubbles, the money is the butcher's. If there are no bubbles, the money belongs to the Jew.

After hearing Yehonatan's brilliant idea, the community leader ran to the judge and told him how to find out who the money really belongs to. The judge thought it was an excellent idea and had his officer bring a large bowl of boiling hot water, and he placed the coins in the bowl. To the judge's amazement, not even one single bubble rose to the surface.

He summoned the butcher, and he interrogated him until the butcher confessed that the Jew never stole his money. The Jew was released from prison, and the city rejoiced for their good fortune. The junior judge had saved all the Jews of Pintshov.

Greater Goes First

When Yehonatan was ten years old, he accompanied his father on a visit to see his father's dear friend Reb Shimshon Wertheimer. A *shidduch* had been suggested with Reb Shimshon's daughter. While visiting, Reb Shimshon took Yehonatan to the king's palace.

The well-respected rabbi and young Yehonatan were given a tour of the palace. They were shown the beautiful rooms full of gold silver and marble. In one particular room was a very large statue covered in gold that went from the floor to the ceiling.

The guide turned to Yehonatan and said, "I heard that you are a very smart boy. Tell me something about this grand statue."

Yehonatan replied, "Our rabbis in the Talmud teach us that we are not permitted to speak in the presence of someone who is greater than them until they speak first. Therefore, let the statue speak first, and then I will respond."

Background: A Jew is not permitted to praise the physical beauty of an idol. The Talmud teaches us that if you are in the presence of someone who is greater than you in knowledge or holiness, you should allow them to speak first. Yehonatan used the word "great" to mean larger in size. With his ingenuity, he was not put in a position to praise the idol but still gave the guide the impression that he considered the statue to be great.

בֶּחָכָם בְּיְהוּדִי

"חֲכָמֵינוּ, זִכְרוֹנָם לִבְרָכָה, אוֹמְרִים, שֶׁחָכָם
אֵינוֹ מְדַבֵּר בִּפְנֵי מִי שֶׁגָּדוֹל מִמֶּנּוּ; וְהִנֵּה אֲנִי כֹּה
קָטָן הִנְנִי, וְהַפֶּסֶל כֹּה גָּדוֹל הוּא — וּבְכֵן, יִפְתַּח
נָא הוּא אֶת פִּיו וִידַבֵּר תְּחִלָּה, וְאָז אָשִׁיב לוֹ
וְאֶעֱנֵהוּ עַל דְּבָרָיו!..."

When Father Enters . . .

Once, when Yehonatan was a very young boy, he was energetically singing and dancing, and his mother asked him why he was being so boisterous.

He explained, "I have been taught that when the month of Adar enters, we need to be very happy. And since we are in the month of Adar, I have to be joyous."

His mother understood. However, she noticed that as soon as Yehonatan's father came into the room, Yehonatan stopped singing and dancing. She asked him why he stopped.

Yehonatan answered, "Our rabbis teach us that, when the father enters, we need to decrease in joy."

Background: The Jewish months each have a name. The festival of Purim falls in the month of Adar. The destruction of the Bet Hamikdash (the Temple) occurred during the month of Av. Our rabbis teach us that when the month of Adar begins, we should increase in joy, and during the month of Av, we should decrease in joy. The actual Talmudic text reads that when the month of Adar enters, we should increase in joy, and when the month of Av enters, we should decrease in joy. The word Av in Hebrew means "father," so the literal translation is, "When father enters decrease in joy." Yehonatan was using a clever play on words.

One Less

When Yehonatan was seven years old, he was sitting with his father at the Purim meal, and his father asked him the following question:

"In the Megillah, we read that Mordechai overheard two of the king's officers, Bigson and Seresh, plotting to kill King Achashverosh. And how Mordechai immediately went to inform the king and tell him that his life was in danger. Achashverosh was the enemy of the Jews, so why did Mordechai want to save his life? Wouldn't the Jews be safer if Achashverosh had been killed?"

Yehonatan replied, "No, Mordechai did the correct thing by running to Achashverosh. This way, two anti-Semites were killed instead of one."

Ma Nishtanah

One year at the seder, Yehonatan's father asked him, "Why do we only ask the Ma Nishtanah, the four questions, on Pesach but not on Sukkot? We do many interesting and strange things on Sukkot—for example, we leave our homes and go live in a hut."

With his brilliant mind, Yehonatan responded that when a Jewish child sees his family living in a hut, he isn't all that surprised; Jews have been persecuted for many years and have had to constantly move from country to country.

However, on Pesach at the seder, Jews behave like royalty, sitting at a table bedecked with the finest dishes and silverware and enjoying freedom. This is something the child is unfamiliar with and therefore cannot hold himself back from asking, "Ma Nishtanah—Why is *this* night different from all other nights of the year?"

The Stolen Afikomen

One year at the seder, when it came time to eat the afikomen, Reb Yehonatan's father realized that his son had taken it. When he asked Yehonatan to return it, Yehonatan said he would return the afikomen if his father promised to buy him new clothes. His father agreed.

הֶחָכָם בִּיהוּדִי

כֶּסֶף מְפָאֲרִים אוֹתוֹ, וּמַטְעַמֵּי חַג עוֹלִים עָלָיו
-- מַבִּיטִים יַלְדֵי יִשְׂרָאֵל בִּבְנֵי עַמָּם וְחוֹשְׁבִים:
מַה זֶּה קָרָה הַיּוֹם לְאַחֵינוּ הַיְּהוּדִים הָעֲנִיִּים,
הַמְּסֻכָּנִים וְהַרְדוּפִים?! וְהַשְּׁאֵלָה מִתְפָּרֶצֶת
מִפִּיהֶם: 'מַה נִּשְׁתַּנָּה?''

After Yehonatan returned the afikomen, his father told him that he would not be giving him any of the afikomen unless he released him from the promise he had undertaken.

Yehonatan removed a piece of matzah from his pocket and declared, "I am eating this matzah for my afikomen." He looked at his father's puzzled expression and said, "I suspected that you might not want to give me my piece of matzah for my afikomen, so I took my piece before I gave yours back to you."

Footsteps

One fine day, Yehonatan's father went shopping with his son to buy them both a pair of shoes. Sometime later, his father noticed that Yehonatan's shoes looked worn out. He showed Yehonatan his own shoes, which were still in good condition. With a smile on his face, Yehonatan said to his father, "It is true my shoes are not in the same condition as yours. Don't you understand for every step you take, I need to take two?"

Sounds Fishy

For breakfast, Yehonatan's father would give him a large slice of herring with bread, and afterward, Yehonatan would go and pray.

One morning, there wasn't enough herring, so his father gave him only the head and the tail, along with a slice of bread. Yehonatan knew this would not be enough for breakfast, and he would still be hungry.

After he finished eating, he began to daven. Instead of praying the full morning davening, he said only Mah Tovu and Aleinu. The davening took him just a few minutes to complete.

When his father asked him how he managed to finish so quickly, Yehonatan replied, "If the head and the tail of a fish is considered to be a whole fish, then by saying the beginning section and the last section of our davening, it should be considered as if all the davening has been said."

The Missing Apples

Yehonatan's father bought several apples in honor of Shabbat. He was concerned that one of the children might eat the apples before shabbat and therefore placed the apples under his pillow.

The next day, he discovered that all but one of the apples had been eaten. He called Yehonatan over and asked him what had happened to all the apples.

Yehonatan responded, "In the Torah, we read that Yaakov had placed many stones under his head before going to sleep. The stones began to quarrel, as each wanted Yaakov to place his head on their stone. Hashem performed a miracle, and all the stones joined to become one stone. Likewise, my dear father, each apple wanted you to place your head on their apple. Hashem performed a miracle, and all the apples became one apple."

Tasting the Fish

Background: We are accustomed to taste the Shabbat foods on Erev Shabbat ito fulfill the verse found in the Musaf Shmonei Esreh *Toameha Chaim Zachu,* which can be understood to mean, "Those who taste [the Shabbat food on Erev Shabbat] merit life." The verse concludes, *"Gedulo bochoru"* [has chosen greatness]. The same set of letters, depending on its vowels, can have more than one meaning and be punctuated to read *Godlo bochoru,* which means "choose the bigger" [portion].

One Friday afternoon, Yehonatan's mother stepped outside for a few minutes. Yehonatan seized the opportunity to run into the kitchen and take a large piece of fish from the pot, which he consumed with great haste. He, of course, did not tell anyone what he had done.

At the Shabbat meal, Yehonatan's mother began serving the fish and realized that the largest piece of fish was missing from the pot. Yehonatan's father knew who had taken the fish and asked Yehonatan why he had taken it.

Yehonatan gladly admitted he had eaten the piece. "You taught me that it is a mitzvah to eat on Friday afternoon from the food that had been cooked for Shabbat. And, by doing, so I will have fulfilled what we say in our davening, 'We should taste the food.'"

His father responded, "You are correct, but the mitzvah is to taste the food, not to eat the largest piece of fish."

Undeterred, Yehonatan replied, "The posuk continues and expressly says, *the large piece.*"

Take the Offspring

Background: *Kinderlach,* in Yiddish, means "little children." It is also sounds the same as a traditional delicacy (kindle cake).

One day, Yehonatan's mother baked a delicacy that was called *kinderlach.* When his mother left the house, Yehonatan ate some of the baked goods. When his mother returned, she noticed that some of the *kinderlach* were missing and asked her son if he had taken some. He said that he had, as the verse says, "You shall send away the mother [bird] and you shall take the offspring [the *kindlach*]."

Hard or Soft Boiled

Background: The word *beitza* means "egg."

Yehonatan's father employed a teacher to teach his son Talmud. The father suggested that he teach him tractate Beitza, which deals with the law of the Yomim Tovim. The teacher told his father that since Yehonatan was such a brilliant boy, he could learn a much more difficult tractate, as Beitza would not be that challenging.

Yehonatan overheard the conversation and said, "An egg can be boiled so that it remains soft boiled, or it can be boiled until it becomes a hardboiled egg. It all depends on the preparation. Likewise, you can learn Masechta Beitza in an easy, superficial way, or you can learn it on a very deep level, and it becomes extremely challenging to learn. It's all in the preparation."

Mind Games

When Yehonatan turned seven, his father felt that he was ready to start learning Talmud and decided he would teach his son all of it from the beginning with Masechta Berachot.

When they reached the section that discusses the topic *hirhur k'dibur domi* (thinking is like speaking), his father said, "I have a question for you. Since we just finished learning the Talmud that teaches us that if I think of something, it is as if I said it. I am not going to actually ask the question. I am just going to think it and you have to answer it."

As quick as a flash, Yehonatan told his father, "I too thought of an answer to your question, and since thinking is like speaking, what do you think of my answer?"

הֶחָכָם בְּנִבּוּרִי

"אַף אֲנִי חוֹשֵׁב לַעֲנוֹת לָךְ, וַהֲרֵי מַחֲשָׁבָה
כְּדִבּוּר הִיא; וּבְכֵן, מַה דַּעְתְּךָ עַל תְּשׁוּבָתִי?..."

Background: In certain situations, a person needs to verbalize a specific statement to fulfill their obligation. There is a discussion whether it will suffice for a person to simply play out the statement in their mind. The discussion centers on whether thought can be considered speech. The conclusion is that thought has the same status as speech.

CHAPTER 3

CHILDHOOD TORAH THOUGHTS

Why Wait to Ask the Question?

Background: Many have the custom when a boy reaches the age of three, he is brought to the cheder. The child is brought wrapped in a tallit to ensure that he does not see anything inappropriate. The teacher then teaches him the Hebrew aleph bet that have been placed on a board and covered in honey. After reading each letter, the boy licks the honey off the letter, thereby impressing upon the child the sweetness of Hashem's Torah.

The aleph bet is comprised of twenty-two letters. Each letter is identified by a name and is pronounced differently, similar to the letters of the English alphabet. Such as the first letter of the English alphabet is identified as the letter a and is pronounced ay.

The Hebrew aleph bet does not have letters that act as vowels. Rather, it has a variety of *nekudot* placed in a specific formation either above or below a letter that indicates how the letter and word needs to be pronounced. For example, the first letter of the Hebrew aleph bet is the letter *aleph*. When a *tzerei* is placed underneath it, the letter is pronounced ay. When a *segal* is placed underneath it, it is pronounced eh.

אָ	אִי	אֵ	אוּ	אוֹ
'a	'i	'e	'u	'o
'aleph + qamatz	'aleph + ḥiriq maleh	'aleph + tzereh	'aleph + shuruq	'aleph + holam
אַ	אִ	אֶ	אֻ	אָ
'a	'i	'e	'u	'o
'aleph + pataḥ	'aleph + ḥiriq	'aleph + segol	'aleph + qubutz	'aleph + qamatz qatan

The name of the seventeenth letter is *pay*, and when pronouncing the letter, it is pronounced *pay*. *Nekudot* placed under the letter *pay* change the way it is pronounced. When a *segal* is placed under the letter it is pronounced *peh*. When a *patach* is placed under the letter, it is pronounced *pah*. Placing a *tzerei* under the letter *pay* serves no purpose.

When Yehonatan was three years old, his father wrapped him in a tallit and brought him to preschool. The teacher was teaching his students the aleph bet.

On the first day, Yehonatan mastered all the letters of the aleph bet and could read the letters forward and backward. The next day, the teacher placed him in the higher class where the boys were being taught the *nekudot*. When the teacher reached the seventeenth letter, he asked his students the name of the letter, to which they all answered in a loud voice *pay* (פ).”

The teacher then asked, “How do you pronounce the letter *pay* if it is vocalized with a tzerei?”

Once again, the students answered, “We still read it as *pay*.”

The teacher then asked, “If so, why do we need to ever place a *tzerei* under the letter pay?”

כֶּחָכָם כְּיִהוּדִי

הוֹסִיף הַמְלַמֵּד לִשְׁאֹל.

קָפַץ יְהוֹנָתָן הַקָּט וְאָמַר לַמְלַמֵּד:

"יוֹדֵעַ אֲנִי אֶת הַתְּשׁוּבָה לִשְׁאֵלָתְךָ, רַבִּי, אַךְ לִפְנֵי שֶׁאֶעֱנֶה, בִּרְצוֹנִי לִשְׁאֹל אוֹתְךָ שְׁאֵלָה".

"שְׁאַל נָא, בְּנִי, שְׁאַל!" — עָנָה הָרַב בְּקוֹלוֹ הַמְלַבֵּב.

שָׁאַל הַיֶּלֶד הַגְּאוֹנִי:

"וְלָמָּה חִכִּיתָ, רַבִּי, עַד לָאוֹת פֵּ"א? וַהֲרֵי יָכֹלְתָּ לִשְׁאֹל אֶת שְׁאֵלָתְךָ כְּבָר כַּאֲשֶׁר לִמַּדְנוּ אֶת הָאוֹת הֵ"א!..."

Now remember Yehonatan was only three, and it was his first day in this class. He said, "Before I answer your question, I would like to ask you a question."

The teacher responded warmly, "Please ask your question."

"Why did you wait to ask your question when we reached the letter *pay*?" Yehonatan asked. "You could have asked your question when we learned the letter *hay*."

Background: Yehonatan was asking his teacher why he waited to ask a very good question until they were learning the seventeenth letter when he could have asked the very same question twelve letters earlier when they were learning the fifth letter.

Would the Real King of Sodom Please Stand Up?

Background: The Torah informs us that the inhabitants of Sodom were extremely evil. Hashem destroyed the city and all its populace.

When Yehonatan was about five years old, he already knew how to daven and knew most of the davening by heart. He also knew many of the Jewish halachot and minhagim. His father decided to hire a teacher to teach him Bereishit. After only a few months, Yehonatan knew the whole sefer by heart. His teacher loved him dearly and enjoyed challenging the young boy's genius.

On one occasion, his teacher asked Yehonatan a trick question, wondering if he could outwit the boy genius. He asked, "What is the name of the king of Sodom?"

Yehonatan answered, "The Torah, in the section Lech L'cha, says that the king of Sodom was a man named Bera."

בֶּחָכָם בִּיהוּדִי

הַקְּטֹרֶת, אוֹתָהּ נוֹהֲגִים אָנוּ לוֹמַר יוֹם יוֹם לִפְנֵי הַתְּפִלָּה: 'מֶלַח סְדוֹמִית רֶבַע'?"

לְמִשְׁמַע הַשְּׁאֵלָה הַ"מַּצְחִיקָה" נֶעֱלַב הַיֶּלֶד, בְּלִבּוֹ הָרַךְ אַף הִתְרַעֵם עַל הַמְלַמֵּד, אֲשֶׁר בִּקֵּשׁ לִטְמֹן לוֹ מַלְכֹּדֶת בִּשְׁאֵלָה שֶׁל שְׁטוּת, אַךְ בִּמְהִירוּת מָצָא תְּשׁוּבָה בְּדֶרֶךְ הַהֲלָצָה וְהֵשִׁיב:

"אָמְנָם שְׁמוֹ שֶׁל מֶלֶךְ סְדוֹם הוּא בֶּרַע, אַךְ כַּאֲשֶׁר הָפַךְ אֱלֹקִים אֶת הָעִיר, נֶהְפַּךְ בְּמַהְפֵּכָה זוֹ גַּם שֵׁם הַמֶּלֶךְ, וּמִ'בֶּרַע' נִהְיָה 'רֶבַע'..."

His teacher then said, "In our daily davening,[9] we state, *melech sedomis Rova*[10]—the king of Sodom was a man named Rova. Was the king of Sodom called Bera, as it says in the Torah, or was his name Rova, as it says in our prayers?"

Background: Homophones are two or more words that share the same pronunciation but have different spelling or meaning. For example, *ad* and *add* or *ball* and *bawl*. Similarly, in Hebrew, you can have two words that share the same pronunciation but have different spelling or meaning—for example, the Hebrew word for "king"[11] and the Hebrew word for "salt"[12] sound the same when pronounced but are spelled differently. Both words have three letters: the first two letters are the same while the third letter is different.

The teacher thought he could outsmart the child prodigy. He was hoping that when Yehonatan heard the teacher quote the prayer "*melech sedomis Rova*," he would mistakenly assume that the word *melech* in the phrase means "king." Thus, the prayer states that the king of Sodom was Rova. When, in fact, the word *melech* in the prayer means "salt." The prayer correctly translates to "the salt of Sodom was called Rova."

Yehonatan responded to his teacher that the king of Sodom's name was Bera[13]. However, when Hashem destroyed Sodom, and He turned it upside down, Hashem also turned the name of the king upside down, and the king's name was changed from Bera to Rova.

---

9. The section called Parshat Ketoret.

10. מלח סדומית רבע

11. מלך

12. מלח

13. ברע

Background: Yehonatan immediately realized that his teacher was trying to trap him by asking a question that made no sense since the tefillah is speaking about salt and not about a king. Yehonatan could have answered his teacher that his question had no basis, as one posuk is speaking about a king and the other posuk is speaking about salt. However, being the brilliant boy he was, he essentially said to his teacher, "Let us imagine that the posuk you quoted actually says king and not salt. I still will be able to explain why there is no contradiction concerning the name of the king of Sodom.

Initially (as seen in the posuk of the Torah) the king's name was Bera. However, after Sodom was destroyed and turned upside down, the king's name was also turned upside down and the letters became rearranged, and the king's name was changed to Rova (as written in the posuk from the davening). The three letters are *bet, reish,* and *ayin,*[14] which spell the word *BeRaH.*[15] Rearranging the same letters spells the word *RoBaH.*[16]

How Many Candles?

It was the eve of the Yom Tov of Chanukah, and Yehonatan and his other classmates were restless and wanted to leave school early. The teacher realized that the boys wanted to go home. He said to them, "If you can answer the following, you can all go home and prepare your menorahs: How many candles do we light throughout the eight days of Chanukah?"

Yehonatan immediately responded by quoting Tehillim 124:7: "The jug[17] broke and we escaped." Yehonatan went on to

---

14. ברע

15. ברע

16. רבע

17. פח "pach"

tell the teacher that if you "break" the numerical value of the "jug" in two, you get 44. He then said, "Now that I have answered your question, we can fulfill the second part of the verse—'and we escaped.'"

Background: The Hebrew word for "jug" has a numerical value 88; we light 44 candles throughout the Yom Tov of Chanukah—on the first night of Chanukah, we light one candle, on the second night two candles, and so on, and on the eighth night eight candles.

The Frogs

Every evening, the Jews of Pintshov would gather in the house of study to learn. There were groups who learned Chumash, others who learned Mishnayot, and other groups who learned Talmud.

One evening, one of the groups were learning Masechta Pesachim and were studying the section (53b) that discusses the plague of the frogs. The Talmud states: *Come and hear: This was also taught by Theodosius of Rome: During the rule of Nebuchadnez-zar [the king of Babylonia] there were three prophets, Chananiah, Michoel, and Azariah. They were given the choice to either bow down to idols or be thrown into a fiery furnace. The prophets sanctified the name of Hashem and chose to be thrown into the furnace.*

The Talmud relates that their line of reasoning was based on the actions of the frogs during the plague of the frogs. The Torah (Shemot 7:28) states, "And the river shall swarm with frogs, which shall go up and come into your house, and into your bedchamber, and onto your bed, and into the houses of your servants, and upon your people, and into their ovens and kneading bowls."

כֶּחָכָם בְּיָהוּדִי

לְמִשְׁמַע דִּבְרֵי הַחָכְמָה שֶׁל הַיֶּלֶד הִתְפָּעֲלוּ הַלּוֹמְדִים, נָשְׁקוּ לוֹ עַל מִצְחוֹ וְהִסְכִּימוּ פֶּה אֶחָד, כִּי יֶלֶד זֶה לִגְדוֹלוֹת נוֹעַד.

The posuk mentions that the frogs entered the ovens and kneading bowls. When are kneading bowls placed near an oven? The kneading bowls are placed next to the oven while they are hot. And even though the ovens were hot, this did not deter the frogs from jumping into the ovens.

The prophets reasoned: A frog is not commanded in sanctifying the name of Hashem, yet they entered the burning ovens, we, who are commanded in sanctifying the name of Hashem, should most definitely enter the burning oven rather than bow down to an idol.

One of the talmidei chachomim studying in the group posed the following question: "How could the Talmud state that the frogs were not commanded in entering the fiery ovens, the posuk specifically states, 'which shall go up and come into your house . . . and into your ovens.' Clearly, the posuk is telling us that the frogs were commanded to enter the ovens of the Egyptians."

The other participants in the learning group offered various answers; however, none of them seemed satisfactory. Yehonatan, who was eight years old, was standing on the side, listening to the discussion. After a while, he couldn't hold himself back and, in a loud voice, said, "I think I know the answer."

The men looked at him, somewhat puzzled, and thought, *How could an eight-year-old boy answer such a difficult question?*

One of the more senior members of the group went over to Yehonatan and said in a sweet, calm voice, "My sweet child, please share with us your answer."

With much self-confidence, Yehonatan shared his answer:

"Yes, it is true the posuk clearly states that the frogs had to enter the fiery ovens. However, it was a command to all frogs collectively and not to each individual frog. Hashem did not command that every single frog without exception must enter the ovens. As such, each frog was within its rights to say to its fellow frog, 'You should enter the ovens, and I will stay in the house till you return. Who said that I have to enter the oven as well?'

"The frogs did not seek a way out. Rather, each and every single frog wanted to be the one to go into the oven and sanctify Hashem's name. Chananiah, Michoel, and Azariah said that we should be inspired by the actions of the frogs. The individual frog was not commanded to enter the ovens, and they still jumped in—we, the Jewish people, who are singularly commanded in sanctifying the name of Hashem, should definitely enter the fiery oven."

The talmidei chachomim were so impressed that such a young boy could answer such a difficult question; they all agreed that Yehonatan would grow to become one of the great Torah scholars of his time.

Honoring His Father

When Yehonatan was ten years old, his father was traveling to the Austrian border and took Yehonatan with him. He was going to visit his childhood friend, the great talmid chochom Reb Shimshon Wertheimer. The two were childhood friends who had learned together as youngsters while living in Frankfurt. Imagine the excitement they felt when they finally reunited after so many years. They spent time reminiscing about what it had been like learning together many years earlier.

During this visit, whenever Reb Shimshon addressed his friend, he called him what he had called him as children. He did not refer to him as Reb Nossan Nota. Yehonatan's father, on the other hand, never called his friend *Shimshon* when addressing him; rather, he gave him the appropriate honor and called him Reb Shimshon.

Yehonatan stood to the side, listening to the conversation between these two great rabbis and became terribly upset by how his father was being treated. Yes, Reb Shimshon was a great talmid chochom and deserved to be called Reb Shimshon, but his father was also a great Torah scholar, and he too should be called Reb Nossan Nota and not just Nossan Nota.

At a certain point, Yehonatan couldn't refrain from interrupting the conversation. He turned to Reb Shimshon and apologized for interrupting without asking permission. He told Reb Shimshon that he was familiar with the Mishnah in Pirkei Avot (Perek 5 Mishna 10) that says, "[There are] seven things [characteristics] in a wise man: one of them being he does not interrupt when someone is speaking."

Yehonatan added, "As such, I should not have interrupted your discussion. However, I am also familiar with the Talmud in Sukkah [21a] that says when two rabbis are talking, even if it is a seemingly mundane conversation, the listener should be attentive to an opportunity to learn from what is being said. As such, I am taking the liberty of interrupting your conversation to make the following observation. From your discussion with my father, I now have an answer to a question that has bothered me for a long time."

"What was your question?" Reb Shimshon asked.

Background: On Shabbos, you are prohibited from writing; if you intended to write the word "goat" and you only wrote the first two letters "go," you have violated the laws of the Shabbos. Even though you wanted to write a word that had four letters and you only wrote the first two letters, it is still prohibited. The reason being the letters "go" spells out a word on its own. The word "go" is a small word that is part of a big word "goat." An example of a Hebrew word that contains both a small and large word would be the Hebrew name Shmuel.

Yehonatan answered, "My question is this: When I was learning Masechta Shabbos [Perek 12 Mishnah 3], it gave an example for the rule of 'writing a small word that is part of a larger word.' The example given is the name Shmuel.[18] The small word is *shm*,[19] whose translation is a name that is part of the larger word *Shmuel*. Why didn't the Mishnah give another example of the small word *shm*[20] from the larger word Shimshon[21]?"

Background: Shimshon is the name of the rabbi who Yehonatan felt was not showing the proper respect to his father.

When Reb Shimshon heard the question, a big smile spread across his face. "That is an excellent question," he said. "Do you have an answer?"

Yehonatan answered, "Yes, I do. Who edited the Mishna?" he asked. "It was Reb Yehudah Hanosi, also known as Rabbeinu Hakodesh and also referred to as simply Rebbi."[22]

Background: In a very respectful manner, Yehonatan wanted Reb Shimshon to realize that he was being disrespectful and should be referring to his father as *Reb Nossan Nota* and not simply calling him Nossan Nota.

Yehonatan continued, "Do you know why Rebbi, the editor of the Mishnah, did not use the name Shimshon? Because Reb Shimshon did not use the name Rebbi."

---

18. שמואל

19. שם

20. שם

21. שמשון

22. He lived from approximately from 135 to 217 CE.

Background: Yehonatan was using a play on words to explain himself. Since Reb Shimshon had forgotten to show respect to his father by not using the title Rebbi, Yehonatan suggested that therefore Rebbi (Rabbi Yehuda Hanosi) had forgotten to use the name Shimshon when giving an example of a small word that is part of a larger word (and used the name Shmuel as the example).

Man-Made Midrash

At a very young age, Yehonatan was renowned for his ability to explain many Midrash (Wonderous Midrash). On one occasion, his teacher in cheder asked the class if anyone could explain the following Midrash Plia[23]: An honest Jew cooks every day, eats stolen foods, and blesses Kadrilomer.[24]" (Bereishit 14:1)

None of the students were able to offer an explanation. After a few minutes, Yehonatan said, "I think I can explain most of it."

Yehonatan took the first letter of some of the words and explained how each letter is the first letter of another word besides the word written in the text. (For example, in English, the word *table* starts with the letter *t,* which is also the first letter of the word *trumpet.*)

Reb Yehonatan divided the sentence into three parts. Part one: The Hebrew for cook is MeVaSHeL.[25] These four Hebrew letters each begin a word that translates to mean "Will be content with what he has."[26] A Jew who is true to his faith will be content on a daily basis with what he has.

---

23. כל מי שיהודי באמת מבשל בכל יום אוכל מן הגזל ומברך כדרלעומר

24. A king during the life of Abraham.

25. מבשל

26. מסתפק במה שיש לו

Part two: The Hebrew word for "stealing" is GeZel.[27] These three Hebrew letters each begin a word that translates to mean "All that happens is for the good."[28] No matter what life will present, he will always declare all that happens is for the good.

Then he said, "Concerning the word KaDReLoMaR[29], I can only explain the first four letters."

Background: The first four letters each begin a word that translates to mean "All that Hashem does is for the good."[30]

A Jew who is true to his faith will bless Hashem for the bad in the same manner that he blesses Hashem for the good, since all that Hashem does is for the good.

Yehonatan said, "I have explained the phrase to mean that a Jew who is true to his faith will be content with what he has. He recognizes that all that happens is for the good since everything Hashem does is for the good. However, I don't have an explanation for the last two Hebrew letters, the letter *mem*[31] and the letter *reish*.[32]"

The teacher responded that the two letters each begin a word that translates to mean, "Rabbinic Midrash."[33]

Yehonatan responded, "I think the two letters each begin a word that translates to mean, 'Our teacher's Midrash.'[34] This

---

27. גזל

28. גם זו לטובה

29. כדרל

30. <u>כל דעביד רחמנא לטב עביד</u>

31. מ

32. ר

33. מאמר רבותינו

34. מדרש רבינו

Midrash Plia is, in fact, a Midrash that our teacher made up on his own and does not go back to the Talmudic era."

The Past Is Past

When Reb Yehonatan was a young boy, he was asked the following question by a non-Jew:

"According to Jewish law, when a non-Jew converts to Judaism, one is prohibited from reminding them that they were once not Jewish. The reason being, you don't want to embarrass and denigrate him by reminding him of his past. Why is it then, when the Torah introduces Yitro, the first convert mentioned in your Bible, does it refer to him as being the priest of Midian? According to your law, it should have simply said his name, Yitro."

Reb Yehonatan responded, "Yitro wanted to convert at a time when it wasn't that fashionable to do so. The Jewish people had just been attacked by the Amalekites, only a few short weeks after escaping Egypt. They had not yet received the Torah, and they did not have a homeland.

"By informing us that Yitro was the head priest of Midian, the Torah is bestowing great praise on him. Even though he had such a prestigious position and the Jewish nation were nomads with no Torah and without land, he was still willing to embrace our faith. This is the reason the Torah informs us that Yitro had once been a priest."

Bar Mitzvah Speech

Tragically, by the time of Yehonatan's bar mitzvah, both of his parents had passed away. His friends made him a bar mitzvah celebration. All the guests were amazed by the brilliance of the words of Torah that Yehonatan shared.

During his speech, Yehonatan elaborated on the rabbinic interpretation of a posuk from the Book of Kohelet 4:13, written by Shlomo Hamelech: *Better a poor and wise child than an old and foolish king.* "Better a poor and wise child" refers to a person's yetzer tov.

Yehonatan asked, "Why is the yetzer tov called a child?" He answered, "Because a person only receives his yetzer tov when he becomes bar mitzvah. Therefore, the yetzer tov is always younger than the person who received it. Therefore, it is called a child. And why is it called poor? Because many people do not listen to it. And why is it called wise? Because it leads the person on the right path."

The second half of the posuk "an old and foolish king" refers to a person's yetzer hara.

"Why is it called a king?" Yehonatan asked. "Because everyone listens to the yetzer hara. Why is it called old? It is called old because it enters the person at birth and remains till the person passes away. And why is it called a fool? Because it leads the person down the evil path."

When he finished his speech, one of the people asked, "My dear bar mitzvah boy, Yehonatan, until today, you did not have a yetzer tov; you only had a yetzer hara. Your yetzer hara was trying to get you to do bad things. How were you able to refrain from doing an aveira?"

The bar mitzvah boy explained, "I would say to my yetzer hara the following: The Torah states 'Hear arguments between your brothers and judge correctly.' [Devorim 1:16] The Masechta

הֶחָכָם בְּיהוּדִי

לְהַשְׁמִיעַ אֶת טַעֲנוֹתָיו בִּפְנֵי הַדַּיָּן הַשּׁוֹפֵט לִפְנֵי שֶׁיַּגִּיעַ הַנִּשְׁפָּט הַשֵּׁנִי."

"בַּהֲלָכָה מְפֹרֶשֶׁת זוֹ" — הִתְלַהֵב הַנַּעַר כִּמְנַצֵּחַ — "דְּחִיתִיו, אֶת יִצְרִי הָרָע, וְכֵן אָמַרְתִּי לוֹ: שְׁתֹק וְהַפְסֵק מִיָּד אֶת שִׁדּוּלֶיךָ, שֶׁכֵּן לְפִי הַהֲלָכָה אָסוּר לְךָ לְהַשְׁמִיעַ אֶת דְּבָרֶיךָ, וְאַף לִי אָסוּר לִשְׁמֹעַ אֶת טַעֲנוֹתֶיךָ לִפְנֵי בּוֹא בַּעַל־הַדִּין הַשֵּׁנִי, הֲלֹא הוּא הַיֵּצֶר הַטּוֹב; רַק כַּאֲשֶׁר יִהְיֶה אַף הוּא נוֹכֵחַ בַּמִּשְׁפָּט, תּוּכַל לְהַשְׁמִיעַ דְּבָרֶיךָ, וְאֶשְׁפֹּט עִם מִי מִשְּׁנֵיכֶם הַצֶּדֶק!..."

Sanhedrin [7b] writes, we learn from the above posuk two distinct laws. The first, a person cannot present his arguments in bet din unless the other party is present. The second being, the judge cannot listen to the claims of one of the litigants unless the other litigant is present."

Background: If there was only one law that neither a plaintiff nor a defendant can present their position in bet din unless the other party is present, there would be no need to have a second law specifically prohibiting the judge from hearing testimony unless both parties are present. Likewise, if there was only one law that a judge was prohibited in hearing testimony unless both parties are present, there would be no need to have a second law specifically prohibiting the litigants from presenting their claims when the other litigant is not present. Since the Talmud prohibits both the judge and the litigants, this clearly indicates the severity of not presenting or hearing evidence when one of the litigants is not present.

"I used this Gemorah," said Yehonatan to defeat my yetzer hara. I would say to it, 'Stop whatever you are saying. You are a litigant presenting your opinion, and I am the judge who needs to decide how I should act. The law is you are not allowed to present your position and I am not allowed to listen to your position until the other party is present. The other party is the yetzer tov. When the yetzer tov will arrive at my bar mitzvah, I will be able to listen to both sides of the argument and then I will decide who is right.'"

Background: The young Yehonatan utilized this line of reasoning to deal with the temptations presented by his yetzer hara.

The Purim Rabbi

Background: The Yom Tov of Purim is full of simcha and joy. Many communities and yeshivas would appoint a Purim rabbi—an individual who would be treated as the rabbi for the day of Purim. The Purim rabbi was expected to say, "Purim Torah" (playfully use far-fetched methods of Talmudic logic to reach laughable conclusions.) To be able to say a Purim Torah, the person had to be quick witted, have a sharp mind, and have the ability to think outside of the box. Original Purim Torah's would bring much laughter to those listening.

Who would be a better choice to be chosen as the yeshiva's Purim rabbi than young Yehonatan? The students of the yeshiva dressed him in clothing usually worn by the town rabbi or head of the yeshiva. He was brought into the yeshiva with great pomp and celebration. All the students were standing out of respect for the Purim rabbi. Yehonatan was placed at the head of the table.

Everyone was very joyous and having a wonderful time. However, last year's student who had been appointed Purim rabbi was extremely upset. He felt he should have been given the honor this year as well. He hatched a plan to once again become the Purim rabbi. He would embarrass Yehonatan, and Yehonatan would not want to continue, and the student body would once again appoint him as the Purim rabbi.

The yeshiva had just begun learning the Masechta Baba Kamma. The previous year's Purim rabbi rose to his feet and said in a loud voice, "It would only be fitting if our new rabbi would share with us an insight in what we are presently studying."

Since the yeshiva had just started to learn the Masechta Baba Kamma, he was hopeful that Yehonatan would have nothing to say, but Yehonatan was not fazed by the request. He announced

הֶחָכָם בְּיַבוּדִי

אוּלָם הַתֵּרוּץ לַקֻּשְׁיָה זוֹ הִנּוּ פָּשׁוּט
בְּתַכְלִית: חֲכָמֵינוּ, זִכְרוֹנָם לִבְרָכָה, אָמְרוּ*, כִּי
הַלַּחַשׁ, אוֹתוֹ יֵשׁ לִלְחֹשׁ לַשּׁוֹר הַמַּזִּיק, כְּדֵי שֶׁלֹּא
יַזִּיק, הוּא: "הֶן! הֶן!" — לְפִי זֶה וַדַּאי אִי
אֶפְשָׁר שֶׁיִּהְיֶה כָתוּב בְּמִשְׁנָתֵנוּ: 'אַרְבָּעָה אֲבוֹת
נְזִיקִין הֵן: הַשּׁוֹר וְהַבּוֹר וְכוּ'', שֶׁכֵּן בְּמִשְׁנָה זוֹ
מְדֻבָּר בְּשׁוֹר הַמַּזִּיק, וּכְשֶׁיִּשְׁמַע הַשּׁוֹר אֶת
הַלַּחַשׁ 'הֶן', הֲלֹא אָז לֹא יַזִּיק!..."

צָחֲקוּ הַשּׁוֹמְעִים לְמִשְׁמַע תְּשׁוּבָתוֹ
הַקּוֹלַעַת וְהָעֻקְצָנִית — וּפְנֵי רַב־הַפּוּרִים
לְשֶׁעָבַר חָפוּ...

* פְּסָחִים קי״ב. ב'

that he would like to share with everyone an original thought on Baba Kamma.

> **Background:** The first Mishna in <u>Baba</u> Kamma lists four situations in which a person's possession causes damage and the owner will be held liable. We have other Mishnayot that also give us listings, such as there are four different Rosh Hashanahs and there are four different types of guardians.
>
> Tosafot points out that there is a slight difference in the language used in the Mishnah in Bava Kamma and in the other Mishnayot. In the other Mishnayot it says, *"There are four Rosh Hashanahs*[35] *. . . There are four types of guards."* While in Bava Kamma, it doesn't write *"There are four types of damages*[36].*"* It leaves out the words *"There are."* Tosafot wonders why, in the case of damages, the Mishna doesn't say, *"There are four types of damages."*
>
> One of the four types of damages is when an ox damages someone else's property. The Talmud in Masechta Pesachim (112b) writes that if you want to stop an ox from causing damage, you should say the Hebrew words *hayn hayn*[37].

Yehonatan rose from his seat and said that he would attempt to answer the question posed by Tosafot. "The answer is very simple," he said. "The Hebrew word for 'there are' is *hayn*. If our Mishnah would have been written like the other two Mishnayot and said, 'There are' four types of damages, it would have used the Hebrew word *hayn*. If we would have used the word *hayn* in the Mishnah, the ox would have heard the word *hayn* and that

---

35. ארבעה ראש השנה הן

36. ארבעה אבות

37. הן הן

would have stopped the ox from causing damage. And we would have only had three types of damages—not four."

Everyone who heard this "Purim Torah" were overjoyed except for one person—last year's Purim rabbi.

Final thoughts: Why is this thought of as Purim Torah? When you are learning the Mishnah in a yeshiva or at home, there is no ox standing next to you that would hear you say the word *hayn* and stop causing damage. The answer given by Yehonatan doesn't answer the question posed by Tosafot, but it is a brilliant Purim Torah.

Second Purim Torah

Background: On the Yom Tov of Purim, we read Megilat Esther. Very often, the Purim rabbi would elucidate posukim in the Megillah consistent with the style of a Purim Torah. The Purim rabbi would expound on a posuk by transposing one of the words with a similar-sounding word that has a different meaning. The Hebrew word for "gather"[38] and the Hebrew word for a "fine"[39] sound the same—*knas*; however, they are written differently. In the Megillah, we read that Esther instructed Mordechai to gather the Jewish people. The verse can be read to mean that Esther placed a fine on all the Jewish people.

Yehonatan asked, "Why did all the Jewish people need to receive a fine?"

---

38. כנס
39. קנס

Background: A father has certain financial rights as it relates to his daughter. These rights are dependent on the age of his daughter. There is an argument in the Talmud (Ketubot 29a) concerning the implementation of these rights. Rabbi Meir is of the opinion that when a fine applies, a sale does not apply—meaning, when a daughter is of a certain age and she is entitled to a monetary compensation, which is set as a fine, such fines are given to the father. During the period of time that entitles the father to receive the fines, he is not allowed to sell his daughter as a maid.

Yehonatan said the answer is obvious: "King Achashverosh had sold the Jewish people to Haman. Queen Esther insisted that every Jew pay a fine. According to Reb Meir, when there is a fine, there is no sale. By Esther placing a fine on the Jewish people, the sale of the Jews to Haman is now voided."

The student who had been the Purim rabbi the previous year jumped out of his seat to challenge him. He asked, "Why did Queen Esther have to follow the opinion of Rabbi Meir?"

Yehonatan was unflustered, and he responded, "Rabbi Meir[40] would recite the Megillah by heart. If you are saying it by heart, the Hebrew words for *fine* or *gather* sound the same. However, when reading it, the Hebrew text clearly states *gather*, not *fine*."

Third Purim Torah

Background: There is a link between Haman and the forbidden fruit eaten by Adam. The forbidden fruit was wheat. *Haman* and *wheat* are synonymous. On Pesach, if you find wheat that had become leavened, you must cover it with an earthen pot.

---

40. Megillah 18b

Yehonatan remarked that since he had shared a Purim Torah based on the teachings of Rabbi Meir, he would share another Purim thought based on his teachings. He said:

"The Talmud [Megillah 16a] relates that Haman's head was full of filth because his daughter had thrown an earthen pot on his head. There is another section of the Talmud [Chulin 139b] that asks the following question: From where in the Torah can one find an allusion to the hanging of Haman? The verse states after Adam ate from the tree of knowledge: 'Have you eaten of [*hamin*] the tree, about which I commanded you that you should not eat?' *Hamin* is spelled in the same manner as Haman: *Heh*, *mem*, *nun*. There is an argument amongst the sages what was the fruit of the tree of knowledge. Rabbi Meir was of the opinion that it was wheat."

After sharing these three sources, he added, "This part of the story took place during the Yom Tov of Pesach. The law is during the Yom Tov of Pesach, if you find chametz products such as bread, you must immediately cover it with an earthen vessel. That will explain why Haman's daughter had thrown an earthen pot on his head."

Background: *Haman* and *wheat* are synonymous; on Passover, leavened wheat needs to be covered with an earthen vessel.

Fourth Purim Torah

Background: There are unique laws of kashrut as it pertains to meat. Beside the meat being slaughtered and prepared in a specific manner, it must also be under constant supervision to ensure that the meat is not swapped with non-kosher meat. If the meat can be identified as being kosher, either by its packaging or the way it is cut, it does not need to be supervised.

After sharing his first three Purim Torah thoughts with his fellow students, platters of various delicacies, including meat, were brought to the tables. One of the students asked Yehonatan if they were permitted to eat the meat since the meat had not been under constant supervision.

Reb Yehonatan replied, "The section of the Talmud [Chulin 95b] that states meats must be under constant Jewish supervision writes that if the meat can be detected as being kosher, even if there had not been ongoing supervision, the meat would still be considered kosher. One of the ways to identify if the meat is kosher is if it is cut into triangles."

Background: The custom on Purim is to eat hamantaschen. The meats brought to the students were meat-filled hamantaschen. Since the meats brought to the students had been cut into triangles, the meat remained kosher and could be eaten.

Queen Esther

Background: Queen Esther requested seven maids, as Megillat Esther 2:9 says, "and the seven maids that were to be given her from the palace." The Talmud Megillah 13a explains that each maid worked for one day; as such, Queen Esther was able to calculate which day was shabbat.

Reb Yehonatan was once asked, "Is it that difficult to know which day is shabbat? Why did she need maid servants to remind her?"

He answered, "Queen Esther had hidden her identity, and no one knew that she was a Jewess. During the week, she worked in the palace, and on the shabbat, she would not work. Her maids would notice this, and they would realize that she was a Jewess. Therefore, each maid worked for only one day. The maids who worked during the week assumed that Queen Esther worked on shabbat as well, while the maid for shabbat assumed that just as Queen Esther didn't work on shabbat, she didn't work during the week as well."

One Test Too Many

When Yehonatan was fourteen years old, he was already known as a gaon. Rabbi Moshe Yitzchak Shapiro, the chief rabbi of Bohemia at the time, was looking for a suitable groom for his daughter. He thought perhaps Yehonatan would be a good match. He decided to check out this wondrous student on his own. He traveled to the yeshiva in Hellishoi where Yehonatan was studying at the time.

When he reached the city, he made his way to the yeshiva, and there he met the young genius. Reb Moshe Yitzchak asked

Yehonatan if he would come with him to one of the houses in the city. He told him, "I am sure you are well aware of the Gemorah in Masechta Pesochim[41] that it is prohibited for a person to marry off his daughter to somebody who is unlearned. I therefore want to test you in learning. I don't intend to discuss sections of the Talmud that I am sure that you are well knowledgeable in. I would like to test you in a totally different way. Let us open any random Torah book at any page and let us see if you can share a new insight into what's written on the page. If you're able to do so, then I am assured that you are a good match for my daughter."

Yehonatan agreed to the rabbi's suggestion. However, in the house they went to, the only Torah book they could find was an old, ripped siddur. Reb Moshe Yitzchak said, "The siddur is also a holy book." He opened the siddur at the section of "Reb Yishmael Omer," a section that lists the thirteen principles of Torah elucidation, and asked Yehonatan if he could share a new insight to this section.

Yehonatan thought for a few minutes and then began to share with Reb Moshe Yitzchak a very deep thought on this section. Reb Moshe Yitzchak was astounded to hear the insights that this young genius shared with him. He was so excited that he hugged him and kissed him on his forehead and said, "Happy is the father who had such a son."

Reb Moshe Yitzchak remained an extra day, and before he left, he met Yehonatan again and said to him, "I would like to ask you one more question before I leave."

Yehonatan answered, "I'm ready to hear another question; however, since I need to be once again examined, then I would like permission to examine *your* knowledge of Torah."

Reb Moshe Yitzchak was not sure why Yehonatan felt that

41. 99a

he now had the right to question him and to discover how much he knows.

Yehonatan saw Reb Moshe Yitzchak's uncertainty and explained, "Don't you understand? You quoted the Talmud that says a person is prohibited to marry his daughter to somebody who doesn't know how to learn, and therefore the custom is that we test the chatan before we announce the engagement. In the same section, it says it is prohibited for a person to marry the daughter of an unlearned person, and in fact, the Talmud says a person should sell all his possessions if necessary to marry the daughter of a talmid chacham."

> **Background:** Just as the father-in-law tests his son-in-law to ensure he is a talmid chacham, the son-in-law should test his future father-in-law to ensure that he too is a talmid chacham. Why, then, doesn't the prospective chatan test his potential father-in-law? There is no need for the son-in-law to examine his father-in-law—as many years prior, the father-in-law had been tested by his father-in-law prior to his own marriage, and the son-in-law can rely on that examination when choosing an appropriate father-in-law.

"However," said Reb Yehonatan, "in my case, you want to test me a second time. The reason is because you were concerned that perhaps the first test wasn't a true indication of my knowledge and that maybe it was an accident that I did well. If that is the case, I too should not rely on the test you received; therefore, I need to test you a second time to ensure that your daughter is indeed the daughter of a talmid chacham."

When Reb Moshe Yitzchak heard this, he smiled. He did not ask Yehonatan any more questions. He knew that his future son-in-law was truly destined to become one of the greatest Torah scholars of the generation.

The Insight

Background: The previous story mentions that Reb Yehonatan shared a very profound insight into the section of Reb Yishmael Omer. This story elaborates on Reb Yehonatan's insight.

Reb Yehonatan asked several questions on this section. Yishmael was the son of Abraham and was considered a very wicked individual. The law is that the names of evil people should be eradicated. Why then was the great talmid chacham and author of this section given the name Yishmael?

Secondly, the style of the Talmud is extremely precise. When two rabbis disagree, and the Talmud mentions both opinions, the Talmud will write "Rabbi A said . . ." and "Rabbi B said . . ." The name of the rabbi is mentioned prior to the word "said." When the Talmud only mentions one opinion or there is no disagreement, the Talmud will write, "Said Rabbi A and Said Rabbi B," where the word *said* is written before the rabbi's name.

Why then in our section where there is no dissenting opinion, does it say, "Rabbi Yishmael said?" The rabbi's name is mentioned before the word "said." The Talmud should have written, "Said Rabbi Yishmael."

Background: The fourth principle is called klal u'prat—A *klal* is a generality. A *prat* is a specification. By way of example, if I say animals and goats in the same context, "animals" is the *klal* and "goats" is the *prat*.

The rule of klal u'prat is applied when the Torah states a generality followed by a specification. When the Torah does this, the intention is to limit the law in question to the specific case. For example, the Torah says regarding korbanot, "from the animals, from cattle and sheep." "From the animals" is a *klal* (general). "From cattle and sheep" are a *prat* (specific). From the principle that a *klal* followed by a *prat* only includes the prat, we know that cattle and sheep are the only mammals that may be offered as a korban.

The fifth principle is called *prat u'klal* – A '*prat*' is a specification and a '*klal*' is a generality. The rule of *prat u'klal* is the opposite of *klal u'prat*. Just as a general category followed by a specific example limits things to the specific case, a specific case followed by a general category is all inclusive and not limited to the specific example. For example, the Torah says regarding the responsibility of a custodian, "If a person gave someone else a donkey, sheep, ox or any other animal to watch..." "Donkey," "sheep" and "ox" are a prat (specific); "any other animal" is a klal (general). This rule is therefore not limited to the three examples provided. It likewise applies to all animals.

There is an argument in the Talmud whether the Torah was written in chronological order. Meaning when Moshe wrote the Torah as dictated to him by Hashem, did he start at the beginning and write it all the way to the last verse? Or did he leave sections blank and filled in those sections when they actually occurred?

Reb Yehonatan stated, "The fourth and fifth principle speak where a general category either precedes or follows a specific example and the laws that are derived as a result. These two principles must follow the opinion that the Torah was written in chronological order, and we therefore can speak in terms of what was written first and what was written later. However, if the Torah was not written in chronological order, then we can't learn any laws based on the principle of what was written first and what was written later. As we don't know what was written first and what was written later."

Reb Yehonatan continued, "We find an interesting discussion in the Talmud. The Talmud writes, Yishmael was the son of Abraham, and even though Yishmael was wicked at the end of his life, he repented and mended his ways. The Talmud deduces this from a posuk describing Abraham's burial. The posuk reads, 'Yitzchak and Yishmael buried Abraham'. The posuk mentions the younger sibling Yitzchak first. Demonstrating that Yishmael, while older, deferred out of respect to his more esteemed brother Yitzchak. This clearly indicates that Yishmael had done *teshuvah*."

He went on, "The fact that Yitzchak's name is mentioned first is only significant if we follow the opinion that the Torah was written in chronological order. However, if it is not written in chronological order, how do we know that Yishmael did *teshuvah*?"

With his brilliant mind, Reb Yehonatan demonstrated how all the questions can be resolved:

"The very fact that one of the greatest Rabbis mentioned in the Mishnah was a man by the name Yishmael is living proof that Yishmael had done *teshuvah*. Because if he had not, then such a great rabbi would not carry his name.

"The only proof we have that Yishmael did *teshuvah* is because the posuk mentioned Yitzchak prior to Yishmael. And Yitzchak's name written prior to Yishmael is significant only if we are of the opinion that the Torah was written in chronological order.

"Reb Yishmael's name was the basis to include in his principles of Torah elucidations of cases where we have a general category and a specific example, and we want to derive laws based on which was written first."

CHAPTER 4

REB YEHONATAN'S PERSONALITY

Tree Top

Yehonatan liked playing with his friends. One of the games they would play was to see who could climb higher up a tree. Yehonatan was always able to climb higher. His father once asked him why this was so. To this, he replied, "My friends always look back, and they become scared when they see how far off the ground they are and need to descend. I, on the other hand, always look up, and I never get frightened."

For Free

Reb Yehonatan never took a salary or a monetary payment for his speeches.

Clothes Make the Man

Reb Yehonatan would wear silk garments on Shabbat, and during the week, his clothing was made from camel hair.

Sleep

Tradition has it that, in his youth, Reb Yehonatan slept no more than four hours during a twenty-four-hour period. He was once asked about the verse that seems to allude that one should sleep for eight hours during a twenty-four-hour period.

Reb Yehonatan responded, "The verse states, 'I would sleep then it would be restful for me.' The Hebrew word for 'it would be'[42] has a numerical value of eight. The verse can be understood to mean, 'I would sleep [8 hours] then I would be rested [and have the strength to continue my Torah learning]. That is why I only sleep four hours a night."

He further added, "The Hebrew words 'for me'[43] has a numerical value of forty. The verse can be read, 'I would sleep [8 hours] then it would be restful for me [for the next 40 hours]."

Was It Immersed?

Reb Yechiel, the son-in-law of the Baal Shem Tov, was once traveling to his hometown in Germany, and he passed by the city of Altona to visit Reb Yehonatan. Reb Yechiel shared stories about his illustrious father-in-law. He said that his father-in-law was able to discern if a vessel had been immersed in a mikvah prior to its use.

When hearing this, Reb Yehonatan commented that this is not so incredible, as he is able to do that as well."

When Reb Yechiel related this back to his father-in-law, the Baal Shem Tov commented, "Yes, a man of his stature, being a great and righteous person, it is indeed not wonderous."

---

42. אן

43. לי

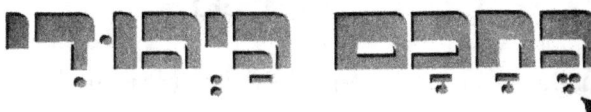

בֶּחָכָם בִּיהוּדִי

בֵּית־הַכְּנֶסֶת הַמֶּרְכָּזִי בְּהַמְבּוּרג

Hamburg Central Synagogue for the Three Communities
of Altona, Hamburg, and Wandsbek

Gold

Reb Yehonatan once remarked that Hashem created gold for the sole purpose of using it in the construction of the Mishkan and the Bes Hamikdash.

Time

Reb Yehonatan would often say that of all that Hashem created, the most precious commodity is time.

Easy and Hard

Reb Yehonatan once posed the following question: "What is the easiest and the hardest thing for man?" He answered, "The easiest thing for a person is to fool himself into believing what he isn't. The hardest thing for a person is to honestly appraise oneself."

Humility

After Reb Yehonatan passed away, his grandson published one of his most famous works—the *Urim V'Tumim*.[44] The Talmud (Baba Batra 175) writes, "Whoever wants to be wise should study the laws pertaining to financial matters." After the printing of the *Urim V'Tumim*, the great talmidei chachomim of Reb Yehonatan's era would add, "And if you want to study monetary matters, then you must study Reb Yehonatan's *Urim V'Tumim*."

---

44. Commentary on Choshen Mishpat dealing with financial affairs.

At the same time he wrote the *Urim V'Tumim*, which would be studied by great talmidei chachomim, he also wrote a very basic book in Yiddish for the less learned that outlined the laws of Shabbat. He wrote, "Even though people may make fun of me because any rabbi could write a Yiddish book on the laws of Shabbat, I don't care as long as I know I am doing what Hashem wants."

The Money Came Back

When Reb Yehonatan's time came to get married, his future father-in-law promised him a dowry of 3,000 gold coins so that he could sit and study Torah without any financial burden or worries. Reb Yehonatan devoted his time day and night to the study of Torah, growing in spirituality and holiness.

One day, Reb Yehonatan's study partner, a very dear and close friend of his, was arrested and thrown into prison. The community began looking for where the prisoner was being held but to no avail. Several days later, the prison warden approached one of the heads of the community and shared the terrible news that the Jew had been placed in hiding and had been sentenced to death.

The guard said if the community would give him 3,000 gold coins, he would help the Jew escape. The community did not have the resources or the financial ability to raise such a vast sum of money in such a short amount of time. However, they felt that they must do their utmost because the Jew was a great rabbi and talmid chochom.

When Reb Yehonatan heard what had happened to his friend, he was worried that the ransom money would not be raised in time. He quickly left the beis midrash, ran home, took all the gold coins he had received from his father-in-law, and handed the money over to the warden. The warden kept his part of the bargain, and no one was the wiser.

The community was unaware of what their beloved rabbi had done, and they were still trying to raise the funds. When the heads of the community came to Reb Yehonatan with part of the ransom money, he told them that he had given away his dowry and that there was no need to collect any more money.

The community was overjoyed, but they insisted that Reb Yehonatan take what they had collected. They explained that redeeming a Jewish prisoner is one of the greatest forms of giving tzedakah. And while they hadn't raised all the money, at least they would have contributed something to Reb Yehonatan's study partner's release.

Reb Yehonatan refused to take any of the money. The fundraisers were extremely upset that they were unable to participate in the mitzvah. They were, however, extremely respectful of their rabbi, and they did not question the decision.

After they left, Reb Yehonatan started having second thoughts. He was worried about how his wife would react when she discovered he had given away their dowry. He imagined that she would become extremely upset, and he would be unable to calm her down. He therefore decided to leave town for a brief period. He hoped that while he was away, his wife would discover that the money was missing, and when he finally returned, she would be more amicable in hearing what he had done with it. He would impress upon her the incredible mitzvah they had both fulfilled and why he handed the money over right away and didn't wait for it to be collected.

Soon after, the priests discovered that the Jew had escaped. They concluded that the prison warden was the one who had released the Jew. They decided that the prison warden would receive the punishment the Jew was supposed to have received.

The prison warden realized that the noose around his neck was getting tighter and he therefore needed to escape as quickly as possible.

Over the years, this warden had stolen vast amounts of gold, silver, and jewelry. He had no idea what he would or should do with it all. He decided that the most trusting and righteous person in the town was the rabbi. He went to the rabbi's house, and he asked to speak with Reb Yehonatan. His wife told the warden that her husband had gone away for a few days.

The warden explained to the rabbi's wife that his life was in danger, he had to flee, and he could not take any of his money with him. He then began to praise the rabbi, saying that he had never met such an upright, noble human being who was willing to give 3,000 gold coins to save his friend. He, therefore, was returning the rabbi's money. He also asked if he could leave the rest of his wealth in safekeeping until he returned—and, if he did not return, then all his wealth would be a gift to the rabbi.

Somehow, not long after he left his wealth with her, the priests tracked him down and killed him. When Reb Yehonatan's wife heard the terrible news, she realized that they had now become extremely wealthy. She anxiously waited for her husband to return so she could tell him the turn of events.

As Reb Yehonatan drew closer to his home, he was extremely worried about what he would tell his wife. When he finally arrived, he was shocked to see that she was overjoyed. She told him that she knew everything that had happened and that the guard had fled and given them all his wealth. She said Hashem must be rewarding him for what he had done. She was sure that he would be as joyous as she was for the gift they had received from heaven.

But that was not the case. Instead, Reb Yehonatan shed tears. His wife asked him why he was crying; Hashem was rewarding him for the mitzvah of redeeming a Jewish prisoner.

Reb Yehonatan said that was precisely the reason he was so upset. A righteous person is rewarded in the world to come. Since heaven had immediately rewarded him for the mitzvah, it means that heaven did not desire his mitzvah. As a result, he cried for a lengthy period.

He decided to fast for three days and then ask Hashem through a dream why He did not want this mitzvah. The answer he received was this: Heaven did not want this mitzvah because he did not permit the community to share in the mitzvah and wanted to do the mitzvah all on his own.

Baron Eybeshitz

While Reb Yehonatan was chief rabbi of Altona, a bishop from Denmark paid him a visit. He had heard of Reb Yehonatan's brilliance and wanted to meet with him. After spending time with Reb Yehonatan, he saw that he was a man of extraordinary brilliance, far surpassing anything he had heard about him.

The bishop had traveled to Altona with the kaiser of Denmark, and he extoled Reb Yehonatan in his presence. The kaiser very much wanted to meet Reb Yehonatan, too. The bishop arranged a meeting between the two. The kaiser was equally impressed by Reb Yehonatan's brilliance. In fact, the kaiser was so enchanted by Reb Yehonatan that he said he would give him anything he wanted.

Reb Yehonatan thanked him for the kind gesture but said he lacked nothing. The congregation looked after all his needs, and he had no interest in worldly pleasures.

The kaiser was insistent that he gift him with something and said he would bestow upon him the title baron. A few days later, an officer arrived with a proclamation stating that Reb Yehonatan would bear the title of baron. Reb Yehonatan told no one of this honor and simply placed the document among his personal files.

Many years later, Reb Yehonatan made a *seudat hoda'ah* (a festive meal thanking Hashem for His kindness) for his immediate family, as he had been successful in defending the Jewish people. At that occasion, he showed them the document and shared the course of events that had led to him receiving the title of baron. They were amazed that he had been able to conceal this from them for so long.

After showing everyone the document, he walked over to the fireplace and threw the document into the fire. He explained that he did so because he was concerned that if his children were to hear that their father was a baron, it might lead them astray in their service of Hashem.

CHAPTER 5

Interaction with Royalty

Pick an Entrance

King Carlos VI and two of his officers were traveling in the king's chariot on the outskirts of Vienna when he noticed Reb Yehonatan walking. He stopped the chariot and called Reb Yehonatan over and said to him, "Rabbi, in your Talmud [Baba Batra 12], it says that a wise man is greater than a prophet. You are a very wise man. I would like to see if you can predict the future. I am about to enter the city, and there are two gates: one is called the gate of the king and the other is the gate of the people. Only the king, his family, and officers can enter via the king's gate. The rest of the population must enter through the people's gate. Tell me, through which gate will I enter?"

Reb Yehonatan took out a piece of paper and wrote his answer on it. He then took an envelope and placed the piece of paper in it and then sealed the envelope. Reb Yehonatan handed the envelope to the king. The king wrote on the envelope that he would not open it until he had returned to the palace.

When the king reached the walls of the city, he stopped the carriage and asked himself, *Which gate should I enter? Should I enter through the gate of the king as I always do? Reb Yehonatan probably guessed that I would enter through this gate, as I am the king.*

He then headed with the chariot to the gate of the people, and before he was about to enter, he stopped. And he said to himself, *I am sure that Reb Yehonatan knew that I wouldn't enter through the king's gate, as that is too obvious. He must have realized that I would choose the gate I normally would never enter.*

He then turned his chariot around to go back to the king's entrance. Each time he was about to enter a specific gate, he got cold feet, and he would go back to the other entrance.

The king then thought of a truly ingenious idea that would solve the problem. He decided that he would make an opening in the wall, and he would build a new entrance through which he would enter. And the king did just that. He was very proud of himself for outwitting the great Reb Yehonatan. When he arrived at the palace, he couldn't wait to rip open the envelope and see which gate had been chosen.

The king was dumbstruck when he opened the envelope and saw that Reb Yehonatan had quoted a section of the Talmud (Pesachim 110), where it states that a king has the authority to break down walls [to make new pathways], and no one has the right to challenge him. The king's respect and awe for Reb Yehonatan increased tremendously, and as a result, he was more favorable to the Jews of Prague.

A Cigar

Reb Yehonatan was very close with the king, who would consult Reb Yehonatan on many matters pertaining to running his kingdom. This created a lot of jealousy among the king's trusted advisors.

Every year, the king would make a large celebration marking his birthday. One year his birthday fell on Shabbat. Of course, Reb Yehonatan was invited. Reb Yehonatan attended out of respect for the king. Of course, he did not partake in the festivities and sat on the side. At a certain point, one of the ministers presented the king with a large chest containing expensive cigars. The king instructed the minister to distribute them to all his guests. Everyone lit their cigars and began smoking around Reb Yehonatan.

One of the minsters whispered into the king's ear that one of his guests was being disrespectful as he was not enjoying the king's gift. The king wanted to know who it was. The minister pointed to Reb Yehonatan. The king summoned him and demanded to know why he was showing such disrespect.

Reb Yehonatan explained that, on the contrary, he was showing the king the greatest respect. He planned to take the cigar home and display it in a prominent place in his home, and whenever he has guests, he will tell them that he was privileged to receive this gift from the king.

Cat-and-Mouse Game

On one occasion, the bishop held a conference with many prominent members of the community. Reb Yehonatan was the representative of the Jewish community. The bishop addressed the audience and stated that, after a lot of research and reflection, he had concluded that there are two driving forces in all of existence—the nature of a thing and the power of the intellect. And he had been trying to resolve which of these was more dominant.

The bishop's advisor stood and stated in an emphatic tone, "The human being is intellectually superior to anything else that exists, and he has the ability to change the nature of anything he so desires."

The advisor pointed to the large table that they were sitting around. "This was once a tree with firm roots in the ground. A human chopped down the tree, and with his carpentry skills, he fashioned this exquisite table." He then pointed to a beautiful gold decanter. "This was a piece of gold buried in the ground. Someone found it, gave it to a goldsmith, and with his wisdom and talent, he produced this magnificent decanter."

The advisor sat down, and the audience gave him a thunderous applause for his brilliant answer. Reb Yehonatan was the only one who showed no excitement.

The bishop saw the lack of response from Reb Yehonatan and turned to him, "My dear rabbi, it seems that you don't agree. Please share with everyone here your position."

Reb Yehonatan faced the audience and said, "I am unable to agree with the bishop's advisor. While it is true that Hashem created the world and when He created mankind, he endowed him with a superior intellect. However, man is limited in what he can accomplish. The human being can never change the inanimate into a living entity. He cannot make vegetation come alive into a breathing, speaking being. Only Hashem is capable of that. The examples given by the bishop's senior advisor was simply taking an existing piece of material and changing its form. The craftsmen did not change the nature of the wood or the gold."

Silence fell on the audience. They were confused; they didn't know who was right. The bishop turned to the crowd and said, "I have heard the opinions of these two great men, and I am not sure who is right. Therefore, I suggest that we all go home, and in thirty days, we will return, and my advisor and the rabbi will have the opportunity to present proof of their opinions and then we will decide who is right."

בֶּחָכָם בֵּיהוּדִי

"לֹא יִתָּכֵן לְשַׁנּוֹת אֶת הַטֶּבַע, וְאַף בְּמַאֲמָץ רַב!" — קָרָא קוֹל אַחֵר.

נִכְלַם הַשַּׂר הַנִּכְבָּד, יוֹעֵץ-הַמְּדִינָה, לְמַרְאֵה מַפַּלְתּוֹ, וְאִלּוּ הַהֶגְמוֹן קָם מִמְּקוֹמוֹ וְלָחַץ אֶת יָדוֹ שֶׁל רַבִּי יְהוֹנָתָן בְּאָמְרוֹ לוֹ:

"אָכֵן צָדַקְתָּ, יְדִידִי! לֹא הַכֹּל נִתָּן לְהַשִּׂיג בְּאֶמְצָעוּת שֵׂכֶל הָאָדָם! מַה דַּל הוּא שִׂכְלוֹ שֶׁל הָאָדָם מוּל חֻקֵּי הַטֶּבַע, שֶׁהֻטְבְּעוּ בַּבְּרִיאָה!!"

Reb Yehonatan returned home to studying Torah and completely forgot about the debate. Some weeks later, as Reb Yehonatan was learning the Talmud, a mouse jumped onto the table. Reb Yehonatan shooed the mouse away. However, the mouse kept jumping onto the table, and Reb Yehonatan had to keep on chasing it away.

Reb Yehonatan opened his tobacco box and took out some tobacco to smell. He then left the box open on the table. The mouse once again ventured onto the table and jumped into the tobacco box. Reb Yehonatan quickly closed the lid with the mouse now caught inside and placed the box into his pocket. Reb Yehonatan returned to his learning. Soon after, there was a knock at the door, and it was the bishop's officer informing him that he needs to immediately come to the bishop's palace as the debate is scheduled to take place in an hour.

Reb Yehonatan had completely forgotten about the debate and thanked the officer for reminding him. When Reb Yehonatan arrived, the reception hall had been set up for a royal banquet. There were magnificent centerpieces on each table. The tables were set with the finest china and silverware. People were eating and drinking and having a wonderful time.

Reb Yehonatan couldn't understand the reason for the celebration. Suddenly, everyone rose to their feet and began to clap, and Reb Yehonatan realized what was happening. At the far corner of the hall, he saw a cat standing on two legs dressed as a waiter and carrying in his front paws a silver tray with a crystal decanter filled with red wine and crystal cups on it.

The bishop and his advisor were beaming; they had proven that a human can change the nature of things. Everyone was witnessing how a cat had become a waiter.

Reb Yehonatan was not sure how to respond when he remembered that the mouse was in his tobacco box, which was in his pocket. He immediately removed the box and opened it. The mouse jumped out and scurried away.

When the cat saw the mouse, the cat dropped the tray and ran after the mouse. The crystal decanter and cups shattered on the ground and the wine spilled everywhere. The waiters spent a long time cleaning up the mess.

People could be heard muttering no matter how much you train a cat, it will always remain a cat. The bishop's advisor was extremely embarrassed by his failure. The bishop walked over to Reb Yehonatan and shook his hand. He then announced, "The rabbi is correct. As smart as we are, we can never change the nature of the world."

Where Are You Going?

While walking the streets of Vienna, Reb Yehonatan was stopped by the king, who asked him where he was going. Reb Yehonatan replied, "I don't know."

The king said, "What do you mean, you don't know where you are going? Who leaves their house without knowing where they are going?" The king thought that Reb Yehonatan's response was disrespectful and had him thrown into prison.

A number of hours later, after the king had calmed down, he thought, *This rabbi is known to be a very wise man. Let me find out why he gave such a ridiculous answer.*

The king instructed that Reb Yehonatan be brought before him. When Reb Yehonatan arrived, the king asked him to explain why he answered in such a disrespectful manner.

In a very calm tone, Reb Yehonatan replied, "I was not being disrespectful. You see, I really didn't know where I was going this morning when we met. My intention was to go to the synagogue to daven. But look where I ended up. I spent the whole day in prison. Therefore, I answered your question correctly by saying I don't know. If you would have asked me, 'Where do you want to go?' I would not have answered, 'I don't know.' I would have told you I want to go to the shul."

Don't Drink Blood

A bishop once approached Reb Yehonatan and posed the following question: "The Torah [Devorim 12:25] prohibits the Jew from drinking the blood of an animal. The verse continues and informs us that not drinking the blood will be beneficial for you and your offspring. Why, by not drinking blood, will this positively impact your children?"

Reb Yehonatan responded, "The reason we are prohibited in drinking blood is because it will cause us to become cruel and callous people. A person's character traits get passed down from one generation to another. By not drinking blood, we are ensuring that our children and grandchildren will not be cruel people."

The Rabbis Are the Guards

The king once asked Reb Yehonatan, "Why is it that when a person transgresses a rabbinic decree, the punishment is more severe than when one transgresses a biblical commandment?"

Reb Yehonatan responded, "What would happen if someone entered your bedroom without permission?"

The king responded, "I would hand him over to the authorities to stand trial."

"My dear king," continued Reb Yehonatan, "what would happen if someone broke into the king's palace with a weapon? What would your guards do?"

"They would kill him," responded the king.

"That," said Reb Yehonatan, "is the reason the punishment for transgressing a rabbinic decree is stricter. The rabbis are like the guards; they need to protect Hashem's laws and punish when necessary. While Hashem can, if He so desires, forgive the transgressor, just as the king has the authority and ability to pardon the intruder."

CHAPTER 6

Anti-Semitism

The Garden

The archbishop of Metz had profound respect for its chief rabbi, Reb Yehonatan, and on one of his visits to Rome, he shared with the pope that their chief rabbi was a man of extraordinary brilliance and intellect. While the pope was no great lover of the Jewish people, he very much wanted to meet the rabbi. The pope considered himself to be a brilliant person, and he was intrigued to meet a person of similar stature.

The archbishop returned to Metz and informed Reb Yehonatan that the pope would like him to visit. Prior to setting out to Rome, Reb Yehonatan was informed that the pope had made a new edict saying that all Jews must leave the city by the end of the year. Reb Yehonatan was extremely worried about the fate of his brothers and sisters.

Once Reb Yehonatan arrived, the pope saw how upset he was and asked him what was troubling him. Reb Yehonatan explained that he had received a question from a Jewish community, and he was struggling to answer their question. The pope asked what the question was, suggesting that perhaps he would know the answer.

Reb Yehonatan shared the following:

"In a distant country, there is a very wealthy sultan who had built himself a magnificent palace, and surrounding the palace was the most beautiful and exquisite garden with trees and plants from all over the world. The sultan took great pride in his garden, and every day, he would walk through to admire its beauty. One day, as he was walking through the garden, he saw that one of the trees had been chopped down. He became extremely angry with the guards for letting this happen.

"He warned them that if this happened again, there would be dire consequences. Several days later, as the sultan was walking through the garden, he saw that another tree had been cut down. He immediately arrested all his guards and threw them in prison."

Reb Yehonatan paused for a moment, and then went on, "It is well known that when there's a problem, the first people you blame are the Jews. So, he called the heads of the Jewish community to a meeting and told them they would now be responsible for protecting his magnificent garden, and if anything should happen to one of his trees, they would be in serious trouble.

"The Jews decided they needed to have security at the main entrance and security surrounding the palace. Perhaps the culprit was not from without but rather from within.

A few nights later, in the middle of the night, somebody left the palace with his head covered and an ax in hand and made his way to another area of the garden and began to chop down a tree. The Jews attacked him and left him lying there unconscious. They ran to the sultan to tell him the good news that they had found the culprit and had dealt with him accordingly.

"The sultan was very excited, and he went running outside with the Jews and saw the culprit lying on the ground. As he got closer, he noticed that the culprit was none other than his only son, the crown prince. The sultan became furious with the Jews and said that they would all have to stand trial for their crime.

"The Jewish community did not know what to do, and they sent an urgent letter asking *me* how to defend themselves in court."

The pope thought for a moment and said, "I don't think the question is all that challenging. The guards were given a task to do; they had no idea who the culprit was. They fulfilled what the sultan had asked them, and therefore they are innocent and should not be punished."

The pope then dismissed Reb Yehonatan.

The next time the archbishop went to Rome, the pope told him that he was not impressed with the rabbi. He said that Reb Yehonatan had shared with him a question that had been bothering him awhile, which the pope himself was able to answer immediately. The pope shared the rabbi's dilemma and the answer he gave.

In a respectful manner, the archbishop informed the pope that, in a sense, Reb Yehonatan had entrapped him. The story about the sultan and the garden had been fabricated. The rabbi wanted the pope to unwittingly admit that he would be doing a terrible thing if he banished the Jewish people from the city. He explained the sultan in the story is Hashem, the garden is the Torah, and the beautiful trees and flowers are the commandments. The Jewish people were given the commandments to fulfill and the responsibility to protect Hashem's laws. And, as the pope correctly said, they did the right thing by attacking the crown prince to protect the garden, as the sultan had ordered. Likewise, the Jewish people were protecting Hashem's Torah by following his mitzvos.

The pope realized that the rabbi had outwitted him, and he removed the decree banishing the Jews from the city.

Fire and Water

Reb Yehonatan approached the king to seek his permission to print the Talmud. The head bishop was at the meeting, and he vehemently opposed the printing of the Talmud. He told the king that there were many sections of the Talmud that were derogatory toward the church. And, furthermore, there were parts of it that were truly foolish.

"For example," the bishop said, "it is written in their Talmud that if someone dreams of a pot, they should anticipate peace and serenity. Now, what does a pot have to do with peace? If the king dreams about a pot, does that mean the king will have peace?"

Reb Yehonatan said, "I will explain: Fire and water cannot coexist; either the fire will cause the water to evaporate, or the water will extinguish the fire. What can bring peace and harmony between fire and water is the pot. When you put a pot of water on the fire, the fire won't consume the water, and the water will not extinguish the fire. Seeing a pot in a dream *is*, indeed, a sign of peace."

And with that, his point was made, and the bishop felt foolish.

Good Business Deal

After hearing Reb Yehonatan's brilliant reply to how a pot makes it possible for fire and water to exist in harmony, the bishop said, "Only *this* Jewish rabbi is smart. If you take any Jew off the street, in one hour, I could convince him to abandon his faith."

The king promptly sent one of his guards to bring the first random Jew off the street. The officer brought in the first Jew he saw. Reb Yehonatan sat back, feeling assured that this man could handle himself.

The bishop said to the Jew, "I am sure it is extremely difficult for you to make a living. Why don't you convert? It would be much easier to make a living. You will make more money and perhaps even be renowned in your community."

The Jew responded, "You've reminded me of my father's final instructions before he passed away. He told me that he made his living by transporting items with his horse and buggy. And that he was leaving them to me, and I too should support myself and my family with his horse and buggy. My father further told me that if someone were to say, 'Let us swap horses and I will also give you money,'" don't accept the deal. Since obviously his horse is inferior; otherwise, why would he be giving you money as well as the horse? However, if the person says, 'Let us swap horses. I will give you my horse, and you give me your horse plus some money,' you should take the deal. Because obviously his horse is better than yours, since why else would he ask for money on top of the horse?" The Jew had nothing more to say.

The bishop was embarrassed for not comprehending the Jew's answer, and he asked him to explain.

The Jew told him, "You wanted that I should swap my religion for your religion, and not only will you give me your religion, you also promise me money and fame. Why would you need to add wealth on top of your religion? The only explanation is because your religion is inferior to mine, and you need to add a monetary incentive. And my father said that is not a sound business venture."

Reb Yehonatan smiled, and the bishop was flustered. It seemed he could not convince the king *not* to allow the rabbi to print the Talmud.

We Are One

Background: The word *adam* is used in the posuk cited to mean "man."

A priest once confronted Reb Yehonatan and challenged him to explain what seemed to be an inditement of the nonbelievers: "The posuk [Bamidbar 19:14] partly states, 'if a man passes away in a tent.' Then, the Talmud [Yevamot 61a] infers that the Jewish people are referred to as men, while the idol worshippers are not. Why are the nonbelievers deemed to be subhuman?" he asked.

Reb Yehonatan responded: "In the Torah, there are four different Hebrew words that mean "man." They are *ish*,[45] *enosh*,[46] *gever*,[47] and *adam*.[48] Three of the four words can be written in the plural, describing more than one person—*ishim, anashim,* and *gevarim.* However, the word *adam* cannot be written in the plural.

"We, the Jewish people, are called *adam* in the singular. Because the world views us as one entity. If a Jew commits a crime, the whole Jewish world bears responsibility, and everyone needs to be punished. When someone not of the Jewish faith does something wrong, not for a moment do we even consider collective responsibility and punishment. Therefore, we cannot use the Hebrew word *adam* to refer to the non-Jew, not because they are not human, but rather because the world views each of them as being independent from the other."

---

45. איש

46. אנוש

47. גבר

48. אדם

Dressed Like Royalty

Well known as the child prodigy of the city Eybeshitz, Reb Yehonatan's fame spread to the city of Prague. Rabbi Zev Wolf Shapiro, who was the chief rabbi of Prague, chose the young Yehonatan to be the future *chatan* (groom) for his granddaughter.

When Reb Yehonatan was fourteen years old, the heads of his yeshiva conferred upon him the title of rabbi. Shortly after, he married Rabbi Zev Wolf Shapiro's granddaughter Elkele and established a yeshiva. At the age of eighteen, he was appointed a rabbi in the city of Prague. Never before in its history had the city elders ever appointed such a young man. However, to become officially appointed, Reb Yehonatan needed the bishop's approval.

The elders went to the bishop, who was amazed that the community wanted to appoint such a young man as a rabbi. The elders encouraged the bishop to examine Reb Yehonatan and stated that the clergy would be equally amazed by his knowledge and genius.

Reb Yehonatan went to see the bishop and conversed with him on many diverse topics. One of the members of the clergy, who was known to be extremely anti-Semitic, became infuriated that this young man was able to answer every question the bishop posed.

In a very disrespectful manner, the clergy member asked Reb Yehonatan the following: "Tell me, Rabbi, where do you get the audacity to stand before the bishop dressed in such a regal outfit? Doesn't your great king, King Solomon, write that a Jew should not glorify himself before the king, and that a Jew should not appear before a king dressed in clothing befitting a person of great importance? [Mishlei 25:6] Our bishop is like a king—he has the authority and power to do whatever he wants."

הֶחָכָם בַּיְהוּדִי

הַבִּנְיָן הַגָּדוֹל שֶׁל בֵּית־הַכְּנֶסֶת הָעַתִּיק ״אַלְטֵנִי״ בִּפְרָג

יֵשׁ מְסַפְּרִים כִּי שֵׁם זֶה נִתַּן לוֹ אַחֲרֵי שֶׁשִּׁפֵּץ — ״אַלְט־נֵי״ פֵּרוּשׁוֹ בְּאִידִישׁ יָשָׁן־חָדָשׁ. וְיֵשׁ הַמְסַפְּרִים כִּי שְׁמוֹ הַמְּקוֹרִי הָיָה ״עַל־תְּנַאי״, שֶׁכֵּן כַּאֲשֶׁר הוּקַם הִתְנוּ מְיַסְּדָיו שֶׁכַּאֲשֶׁר תַּגִּיעַ הַגְּאֻלָּה וְעַם יִשְׂרָאֵל יָשׁוּב לְאַרְצוֹ יַעֲבִירוּ אֶת הַבִּנְיָן כֻּלּוֹ לִירוּשָׁלַיִם.

The Ancient Synagogue's Building "Altnei"

There are those who suggest that the Synagogue's name was given after it had been repaired and upgraded. *Altnei* is in fact, two Yiddish words, *Alt* and *Nei*, that mean *old* and *new*, meaning the Synagogue was once old but now it is like new.

Another theory for the name *Altnei* is, in fact, two Hebrew words, *Al Tnai*, that translated mean *on condition*, meaning that the Synagogue was built in the city of Prague *on the condition* that when Moshiach will come it will be transported to Jerusalem.

הֶחָכָם בַּיְהוּדִי

"שְׁתֵּי הַשְּׁאֵלוֹת אֲשֶׁר שָׁאַלְתָּ, מִתְרַצּוֹת
אַחַת בַּחֲבֶרְתָּהּ: מִכֵּיוָן שֶׁחֲכָמֵינוּ, זִכְרוֹנָם
לִבְרָכָה, אָמְרוּ, שֶׁיָּאָה הָעֲנִיּוּת לַיְּהוּדִים, הֲרֵי
הָעֲנִיּוּת הִנָּהּ הֲדָרָם וְהוֹדָם, וְלָכֵן לֹא יָכֹלְתִּי
לָבוֹא אֶל הַמֶּלֶךְ בְּבִגְדֵי עֲנִיּוּת, שֶׁכֵּן לוּ עָשִׂיתִי
כָּךְ, הָיִיתִי עוֹבֵר עַל עֵצַת שְׁלֹמֹה הַמֶּלֶךְ בְּסֵפֶר
מִשְׁלֵי: 'אַל תִּתְהַדַּר לִפְנֵי מֶלֶךְ', שֶׁהֲרֵי דַּוְקָא
בִּגְדֵי הָעֲנִיּוּת הֵם הֵם בִּגְדֵי הֶהָדָר שֶׁלָּנוּ,
הַיְּהוּדִים; אָכֵן מֵעַתָּה תָּבִין, מַדּוּעַ הִתְלַבַּשְׁתִּי
בַּבְּגָדִים הַנָּאִים שֶׁעָלַי..."

The clergyman didn't wait for an answer and said, "And I have another question, and this time I am going to quote a section of your Talmud, where it states that the glory of a Jew is when he is poor [Chagigah 9b]. Why did you then dress in such fancy and expensive clothing when you should have dressed as a pauper?"

Reb Yehonatan always remained calm and never got angry. This occasion was no exception. He said, "I want you to know that your two questions are actually one question with one answer. And you answered your own question."

The clergyman grew red in the face, waiting for Reb Yehonatan to explain.

"As you correctly quoted," he said, "the Talmud *does* say that our glory is when we are poor, and I should have dressed in clothes worn by a pauper. However, I thought to myself, *How can I stand before the bishop dressed in clothes befitting a pauper?* Doesn't King Solomon write that we are not allowed to glorify ourselves before a king? And if I would wear clothes of a poor man, I would be glorifying myself before the king. I therefore had no choice but to dress in clothing fit for a prince."

Walking Stick

The bishop wanted to make life difficult for Reb Yehonatan, so he gave him a gift of an expensive cane with a cross affixed to the top.

Reb Yehonatan knew that if he *didn't* use the cane, the bishop would use it as an excuse to unleash fiery anger at him. He also knew that if he *did* use the cane, he would be denigrating the Jewish faith. He wasn't quite sure what to do. However, the very next day, Reb Yehonatan went for a walk using the cane.

Upon seeing him in the street, the bishop ran over to see if he was using the cane he had given him. Indeed, Reb Yehonatan was using the cane, but Reb Yehonatan had cut the top off the stick. The cross had been removed.

The bishop was enraged. "How dare you denigrate my faith!" he shouted.

Reb Yehonatan held up his hand. "Nothing could be further from the truth," he said calmly. "The cane was simply too long for my height and needed to be shortened."

The bishop's face distorted with confused fury. "When you shorten a stick, you shorten the part that touches the ground!"

Reb Yehonatan said, "On the contrary, the bottom part reached the ground perfectly; it was the upper part that reached beyond my hand."

Mishloach Manot

Background: One of the mitzvos on Purim is to send *mishloach manot* (gifts of food items to one's friends).

A certain bishop despised Reb Yehonatan immensely, and he would seek out ways to cause him pain and grief. One year, prior to the Yom Tov of Purim, the bishop decided to send Reb Yehonatan *mishloach manot*. He prepared a beautiful tray of fruit, and on the top of the fruit, he placed a picture of a pig.

He instructed his servant to personally deliver it into the hands of Reb Yehonatan. The bishop couldn't wait to hear from his servant how Reb Yehonatan reacted. More than likely, he would start screaming and become terribly angry or he would take the whole tray and throw it into the garbage. Or maybe he would send it back in disgust.

When the servant returned, he was carrying the same tray of fruit but with a picture of Reb Yehonatan on top. The bishop asked the servant what had happened.

The servant said that Reb Yehonatan calmly stated that it was tradition to reciprocate and send *mishloach manot* back. Therefore, he was returning the gift with a minor change. He had removed the picture of the pig and replaced it with a picture of himself.

When the bishop asked why Reb Yehonatan had done this, the servant replied that Reb Yehonatan had said, "Since the bishop sent me a picture of himself on top of the fruit, I too will place a picture of *myself* on top of the fruit."

Forgive and Forget

Background: Megillat Esther records that Haman wanted to wipe out the Jewish people; Haman and his ten sons were hung from the gallows.

A certain bishop, who we know was a terrible anti-Semite, once asked Reb Yehonatan, "According to your Bible, you are not allowed to take revenge or bear a grudge. Why after so many thousands of years do you still remember what Haman wanted to do to the Jewish people?"

Reb Yehonatan responded, "We are not reflecting and remembering the actions of the arch villain Haman; rather, we are declaring to the Hamans of each generation that if you continue to follow in Haman's footsteps, you will suffer the same fate."

To Bribe or Not to Bribe

An anti-Semite once approached Reb Yehonatan and asked him the following: "In your Torah, it clearly states that a judge is not permitted to take a bribe from one of the litigants. Why is it that when a Jew has a court case with a non-Jew, very often the Jew will bribe the judge?"

Reb Yehonatan responded, "The reality is most of the judges are anti-Semites, and when they have to try a case between a Jew and a non-Jew, the judge will automatically favor the non-Jew. When the Jew bribes the judge, he is simply placing himself on an even playing field with the non-Jew."

Lack of Decorum

The local bishop once asked Reb Yehonatan, "Why is it that when you walk into a shul or house of study, there are times when the congregants are not being respectful, and there seems to be a lack of decorum?"

Reb Yehonatan, who always defended his people, responded in the following manner: "My dear bishop, our Torah says that we are Hashem's children, and the shul is Hashem's home. A guest or a stranger in Hashem's home will be on their best behavior, while Hashem's children are in their own home when they are in the shul, and sometimes, children are not on their best behavior at home."

Blood Libel

Background: During the Middle Ages, anti-Semites would accuse the Jewish people of baking the matzah for the Yom Tov of Pesach using the blood of a non-Jewish child.

While Reb Yehonatan was the rabbi of Prague, a non-Jewish child was missing and presumed to be dead. Several people accused the Jews of killing the child and using the blood to bake matzah. The bishop instructed Reb Yehonatan to appear the next day to explain their actions.

That night, the bishop couldn't sleep, and he was pacing on his balcony. He noticed in the distance two men carrying a sack. He was intrigued, so he followed them into the forest and saw them hide a sack. The bishop knew that they were not Jewish and confronted them. They admitted they had killed the child and were trying to dispose of the body before it was discovered.

The next day, Reb Yehonatan appeared at the bishop's home, unaware that the Jewish people had nothing to fear. The bishop asked him to explain the posuk, "Behold the Guardian of the Jewish people does not slumber or sleep."

Reb Yehonatan explained it to mean that Hashem does not slumber or sleep because He is always protecting the Jewish people.

The bishop asked, "Why does the posuk say that Hashem doesn't sleep or slumber? It is repetitive." The bishop did not wait for a response and said, "Hashem does not slumber, and He also doesn't let others sleep because He is protecting the Jewish people. Last night, as much as I tried, I couldn't sleep, and since I was up, I saw the real culprits trying to dispose of the body, and as a result, I now know that the Jews of Prague did not commit such a hideous crime."

הֶחָכָם הַיְּהוּדִי

לֵךְ, אֲדוֹנִי הַשַּׂר!" — נַעֲנָה לוֹ ר' יְהוֹנָתָן,
כְּשֶׁעַל פָּנָיו נָסוּךְ חִיּוּךְ רָחָב.

"וְהֵיכָן הוּא אוֹתוֹ מָקוֹם נִפְלָא, רַבִּי??"
— שָׁאַל הַשַּׂר בְּקֹצֶר־רוּחַ.

"בְּבֵית־הַקְּבָרוֹת שֶׁלָּכֶם!..." — הָיְתָה
הַתְּשׁוּבָה.

Where There Are No Jews

When Reb Yehonatan was living in Metz, one of the princes of the city was a terrible anti-Semite. The prince was walking in the street and reflecting on how the Jewish population was increasing, and soon, there would be more Jews than gentiles in his city. This made him extremely angry.

As he was getting angrier and angrier, he saw the chief rabbi, Reb Yehonatan, walking past. He screamed out angrily, "Rabbi, your people will soon overrun my city! I have to escape. I will pay someone a lot of money if they can tell me where I can go so I will not have to live together with Jews."

With a broad smile, Reb Yehonatan responded, "I will tell you, and I will not even charge you a penny."

The prince asked, "Where is this place? I need to know."

"You should take up permanent residence in your cemetery," Reb Yehonatan told him. "You will not find any Jews there."

At Your Wedding

Reb Yehonatan served as the head of the bet din in Metz, France, and he was very well liked by the head cardinal. The cardinal once invited him for a meal. He wanted Reb Yehonatan to have a pleasant experience and ensured that all the food was kosher and that all the eating utensils were kosher. However, the cardinal had also invited the local bishop, who despised Reb Yehonatan.

The bishop was seated at the table and saw how much the cardinal liked the rabbi, which made him extremely angry and envious. He wondered to himself what he could do to ridicule and make fun of the rabbi. The bishop thought of an idea. He excused himself and secretly arranged for one of the waiters bring pig's meat to the table and place it before Reb Yehonatan.

When the food arrived along with the platter of pork, the bishop said to Reb Yehonatan, "You must eat this meat! It tastes wonderful, and it is very healthy for you!"

Reb Yehonatan did not show his intense anger and calmly asked the bishop, "Don't you know that we Jews are prohibited from eating the meat of a pig?"

With an impatient tone, the bishop asked, "Rabbi, will there ever be a time when the two of us will be able to eat pig's meat from the same platter?"

"Of course," answered Reb Yehonatan, "at your wedding."

Background: According to church laws, a bishop is not permitted to marry. Reb Yehonatan essentially said, "We will never eat pig together since you will never marry."

Stand or Sit? That Is the Question

A certain priest, who was a dreadful anti-Semite, once approached Reb Yehonatan with the following statement; his words were laced with venom: "I have been told that you Jews are very respectful of your rabbis, and when you see a rabbi, you stand up to show respect."

Reb Yehonatan responded, "Indeed that is correct."

The priest then asked, "I have also been told that when a Jew sees a barking dog running toward him, the Jew will sit on the ground."

"Again, you are correct," the rabbi responded.

"If that is the case," the priest asked, "what happens when a Jew is confronted by a rabbi *and* an angry dog? What do you Jews do—do you stand or sit?"

"My dear priest, that is a very good question," Reb Yehonatan replied. "I am unsure of how to answer it correctly. Whenever we rabbis are uncertain, we follow a specific protocol: We see how the Jewish people conduct themselves, so what I suggest is that we take a walk together. Let us see whether my people stand or sit when they see me, the rabbi, walking with you."

The Fence

Reb Yehonatan was once standing in his backyard. His neighbor, who always unleashed anti-Semitic remarks whenever he saw the rabbi, was also standing in his own backyard. The men were separated only by a fence.

The neighbor started conversing with Reb Yehonatan in a false friendly manner but then quickly began making fun of him and ridiculing Jewish people, as was usual. Finally, with his fists clenched, he asked, "What is the difference between a Jew and a pig?"

Reb Yehonatan, who always remained calm, pointed between them and said, "Right now, the difference between a Jew and a pig is this fence separating *me* from *you*."

בֶּחָכָם כְּיָבוּדִי

שֶׁלֹּא פִּלֵּל, כַּנִּרְאֶה, לִשָׁמְעָה מִפִּיו שֶׁל רַב יְהוּדִי
— וַיֵּלֶךְ לוֹ מְבֻיָּשׁ וַחֲפוּי־רֹאשׁ...

★

The Table

An anti-Semite sat at a table across from Reb Yehonatan and asked, "Tell me, rabbi, what is the difference between a dog and a Jew?"

As quick as a flash, Reb Yehonatan responded, "The length of this table."

You Are What You Eat

Background: Jewish law prohibits cooking meat and milk together.

A minister once asked Reb Yehonatan the following question: "You Jews consider yourselves to be very smart people. Why then do you keep laws that make absolutely no sense? I will give you an example. Imagine you have a hen and you feed it butter and milk. The hen when slaughtered is kosher to be eaten. On the other hand, if you are cooking a chicken on the stove and milk falls into the pot, the chicken is no longer kosher. Don't you see how illogical your laws are? They make no sense, so why do you keep them?"

Reb Yehonatan began to laugh and said to the minister, "You do exactly the same thing—and let me explain. You have no problem eating pig's meat even though just before it was killed the pig may have just eaten rotten and disgusting foods. However, if the pig's meat is cooking in a pot and some dirt or rotten food falls into the pot, you will throw away everything in the pot. From our perspective, when milk falls into a pot of meat, it would be the same as if rotten food or garbage had fallen into the pot of meat."

הֶחָכָם בְּיֹ֫ובֵּ֫רִי

"לָמָה זֶה תִּתְמַהּ? וַהֲלֹא אַף אַתֶּם, בְּנֵי
אֻמּוֹת הָעוֹלָם, נוֹהֲגִים בְּדוֹמֶה:

חֲזִיר, הָאוֹכֵל לִכְלוּךְ וְטֻנֹּפֶת — אַף עַל
שֻׁלְחֲנוֹת מְלָכִים יַעֲלֶה, וְאִלּוּ חֲזִיר, הַמִּתְבַּשֵּׁל
בְּסִיר, מִשֶּׁנּוֹפֵל לְתוֹכוֹ מַשֶּׁהוּ טֻנֹּפֶת — הֲרֵי
נַעֲשָׂה הוּא מָאוּס בְּעֵינֵיכֶם עַד מְאֹד!..."

★

Drink This

One of the ministers in Vienna, who was no friend of the Jews, once approached Reb Yehonatan.

"My esteemed rabbi," he said, "I would like to ask you a question. In your Torah, it says you are not allowed to eat worms. I can understand that not everyone likes those little creatures. However, I recently discovered something rather strange: if the worm is still in the fruit, you *can* eat the fruit and the worm, but once the worm has left the fruit and is now on the table, your Torah does not allow you to eat it."

Reb Yehonatan remained silent; the minister had not yet asked his question.

"Can't you see how foolish this law is?" the minister finally asked. "If you can't eat worms, then even if it is still in the fruit, you shouldn't be able to eat it. And if you can eat worms, then even if it is on the table, you should be able to eat it."

Reb Yehonatan asked the minister for a cup. With the cup in hand, he said to him, "My dear minister, I would like you to do me a small favor. It may seem strange, but I will soon explain why I have asked you."

"It would be my pleasure," said the minister.

"I would like you to spit into the cup." Reb Yehonatan placed the cup on the table, and the minister obliged and spat into the cup. "Now, I would like you to pick up the cup and drink your saliva," Reb Yehonatan said.

"Most definitely not," said the minister, crossing his arms and taking a step back. "How can I drink spit?"

"I don't understand," said Reb Yehonatan. "Just a second ago, the spit was in your mouth, and you were not repulsed by it. Why should it make any difference now that it is in a cup?"

Reb Yehonatan didn't wait for the minister to respond and said, "The same thing is with the worm. While it is in the fruit, you wouldn't find eating it disgusting; however, once it is no longer in the fruit, you wouldn't be able to eat it."

בֶּחָכָם בִּיהוּדִי

צִוָּה ר׳ יְהוֹנָתָן עַל הַשַּׂר לִבְלֹעַ אֶת רֻקּוֹ —
אַךְ הַלָּה מֵאֵן לַעֲשׂוֹת זֹאת בְּהַסְבִּירוֹ כִּי הַדָּבָר
מָאוּס עָלָיו.

"וַהֲלֹא רֻקְּךָ הוּא זֶה, אֲשֶׁר רַק לִפְנֵי רֶגַע
קָט הָיָה בְּפִיךָ, וְלֹא עוֹרֵר בְּךָ כָּל הַרְגָּשַׁת גֹּעַל
— וּמַדּוּעַ נִמְאָס הוּא בְּעֵינֶיךָ עַתָּה?" — כָּךְ
שָׁאַל ר׳ יְהוֹנָתָן שֶׁלֹּא עַל-מְנָת לְקַבֵּל תְּשׁוּבָה,
וְהוֹסִיף לְהַסְבִּיר: "הוּא הַדָּבָר! כָּל עוֹד נִמְצָאוֹת
הַתּוֹלָעִים בַּמַּאֲכָל — הֵן אֵינָן מְאוּסוֹת, וְלָכֵן
מֻתָּרוֹת הֵן בַּאֲכִילָה, מַה שֶּׁאֵין כֵּן לְאַחַר הַפְּרִדָן
מִמֶּנּוּ!"

You Win

Reb Yehonatan was very much beloved by the king, which enraged the local bishops. A delegation of bishops, led by the senior bishop, requested an audience with the king. The senior bishop requested that he be permitted to summon Reb Yehonatan to a public debate about which faith is superior.

Well aware of Reb Yehonatan's brilliance, the king refused. "You will lose, and it will be a terrible embarrassment," he said.

However, the bishop was confident that he wouldn't lose. And when he did win, he said he would force Reb Yehonatan and all the Jewish people to convert. The bishop was so adamant and persuasive that he finally convinced the king to permit the debate.

The king summoned Reb Yehonatan and informed him that the head bishop was to debate him. Reb Yehonatan refused. However, the king was insistent.

On the day of the debate, Reb Yehonatan was brought to a large hall. There were two chairs placed at the front—one for Reb Yehonatan and one for the bishop. The hall was full of people who anxiously awaited for the debate to commence.

The king instructed the bishop to begin. The bishop, in turn, requested that Reb Yehonatan start.

Reb Yehonatan took the bishop aside and said, "If we are to debate about which faith is superior, I will demonstrate why my faith is true, and you will explain why your faith is true. It will not be interesting or exciting and neither of us will get our point across. I suggest a different format: You explain why your religion is inferior and why my faith is the true faith, and I will do the same. This will keep the audience interested."

The bishop thought it was a brilliant idea and told Reb Yehonatan to go first. Reb Yehonatan said it would be disrespectable for him to begin, and he insisted the bishop start.

The bishop rose and, in a loud voice, pointed out all the inconsistencies in his faith, extolling the Jewish religion in the process. The bishop concluded and took his seat.

The audience was dumbfounded; they had not been made aware of the rules of the debate. The king turned to Reb Yehonatan and told him it was his turn to address the crowd.

Reb Yehonatan stood, looked at the crowd and at the bishop, and declared, "There is nothing I can muster as a response. Everything the bishop said is the truth."

The king was furious with the bishop, screaming at him that he had warned him he could never defeat the rabbi in a debate. The king's admiration and respect for Reb Yehonatan increased tenfold that day as a result.

Angels in Heaven

Reb Yehonatan was often confronted by priests who enjoyed making fun of and ridiculing the Jewish religion. In one case, Reb Yehonatan was accosted by a priest and challenged with the following question: "My dear rabbi, you and your people believe that our religion has no basis to it. How could so many people make such a terrible mistake to believe in something that is not true?"

Reb Yehonatan listened attentively and then said, "I will respond in three days' time."

Three days later, while the priest was out walking, he noticed Reb Yehonatan standing across the street, staring with great intensity up at the sky. The priest walked over and asked Reb Yehonatan, "What are you looking at?"

Reb Yehonatan answered, "Can't you see?"

"See what?"

"In the sky? Can't you see all the angels, carrying harps, singing, and dancing in heaven?"

The priest looked up and didn't see anything. However, he was too embarrassed to admit he couldn't see the angels and told Reb Yehonatan, "Oh, of course I see them. It is truly majestic!"

As people walked by, they saw the rabbi and the priest staring into the sky. They wanted to know what the priest and rabbi were looking at.

"Can't you see all the angels in the sky? We can't take our eyes off them," the priest replied.

The people, of course, did not see anything, as there was nothing to see. However, they were too embarrassed to admit it and feared that the priest would take it as a sign that they were sinners who were unworthy of seeing the angels. They therefore shouted with glee, "Yes, we see them as well!"

By that time, a large crowd had gathered. They were all gazing in wonder at the invisible angels.

Reb Yehonatan tapped the priest on the shoulder and asked that he walk with him to the corner. Once out of earshot, he said to the priest, "You know I was jesting. There are no angels playing the harp and dancing in the sky."

"I know there are no angels," the priest admitted. "I hope you will not make fun of me for pretending to see the angels."

"Now you see the truth," said Reb Yehonatan. "You and I both know there are no angels, but look at all those fools over there pretending to see what doesn't exist. It makes absolutely no difference how many people say they are seeing angels, *we* know the truth."

The priest understood what Reb Yehonatan had set out to prove. He acknowledged that Reb Yehonatan was right and that he had been wrong; it did not matter how many people said something was true if the truth was known to be false.

Look Me in the Eye

Reb Yehonatan had to meet the government-appointed censor whose role was to ensure that all publications and letters were not antigovernment.

Knowing this censor was an evil anti-Semite, Reb Yehonatan would not look at the man's face since the Talmud states that it is prohibited to look at the face of a wicked person.

As they spoke, the censor realized that Reb Yehonatan was not looking at him and became upset. Wanting to impress the rabbi with his knowledge, he said, "Why don't you look at my face? Even your forefather Yaakov looked at the face of his brother Esau, who was extremely wicked. I know this to be the case because in your Torah, it says, 'I have seen your face.' And the verse is telling us that Yaakov looked at the face of Esau. So, tell me, why can't you look at *my* face?"

"Do you remember the second part of the verse?" Reb Yehonatan asked, still averting his eyes.

"Of course, I do," responded the censor. "The verse says, 'which is like seeing the face of Hashem.'"

"Ah," said Reb Yehonatan. "Let us study the whole posuk together. The verse reads 'I have seen your face which is like seeing the face of Hashem.' My forefather Yaakov was a very righteous and holy man. Do you really believe Yaakov is saying that the face of Esau is like the face of Hashem? Of course not. You simply misunderstood. Let me explain what my forefather said: Yaakov told his wicked brother that just as we cannot see Hashem, likewise he cannot see his face, as he is wicked . . . Similarly, I cannot see your face."

הֶחָכָם בִּיהוּדִי

"הַאִם יִתָּכֵן, לְדַעְתְּךָ, שֶׁיַעֲקֹב אָבִינוּ,
הַצַּדִּיק וְהַתָּמִים, יְדַמֶּה, חַס וְשָׁלוֹם, אֶת עֵשָׂו
— לְהַבְדִּיל אֶלֶף אַלְפֵי הַבְדָּלוֹת — לְהַקָּדוֹשׁ־
בָּרוּךְ־הוּא — מֶלֶךְ מַלְכֵי הַמְּלָכִים?!" —
שָׁאַל רַבִּי יְהוֹנָתָן שֶׁלֹּא עַל־מְנָת לְקַבֵּל תְּשׁוּבָה
— "אֶלָּא כְּשֵׁם שֶׁאֵין בְּאֶפְשָׁרוּתוֹ שֶׁל אָדָם
לִרְאוֹת אֶת הַשֵּׁם יִתְבָּרַךְ, כְּמוֹ שֶׁכָּתוּב: '... לֹא
יִרְאַנִי הָאָדָם וָחָי', כֵּן יַעֲקֹב אֵינוּ יָכוֹל לְהִסְתַּכֵּל
בְּפָנָיו שֶׁל עֵשָׂו!..."

Greetings

Reb Yehonatan often visited the king, with whom he was close, at his palace. On one occasion, as they were walking together, they passed by a large statue. Out of respect, all those who would pass would take off their hat.

The king noticed that Reb Yehonatan did not remove his hat. The king was troubled by Reb Yehonatan's lack of respect and asked him why he didn't take off his hat.

Reb Yehonatan replied, "I only greet those who will greet me in turn."

Can't Change the Law

On one occasion, a group of priests went to see Reb Yehonatan with what they believed to be a valid complaint. They said, "Why is it that you consider us to be impure? We know it is true because you don't let us drink your wine. In fact, you don't even let us *touch* your wine."

Reb Yehonatan responded, "The Church acts no differently than we do. Isn't it the practice of the Church that if the heads of the Church gather and enact a new decree, it becomes binding on all their faithful? The decree can only be reversed and nullified if the heads of the Church deem so."

The priests nodded their understanding, and Reb Yehonatan continued, "Likewise, the prohibition of a gentile from drinking or touching our wine was enacted by our great and righteous prophets, Daniel, Chananiah, Michoel, and Azariah. How then can we come along and permit what these great prophets had prohibited?"

The priests accepted Reb Yehonatan's explanation and did not bring up this issue again.

Horse or Donkey

A certain prince who was a fanatical anti-Semite once asked Reb Yehonatan, "Tell me, Rabbi, why do you Jews act in such a haughty manner? You ride on horses and travel in carriages while your greatest leader Moshe rode a donkey, and your Messiah will also appear riding on a donkey?"

"Thank you for your question," responded Reb Yehonatan. "Let me explain: The reason we ride horses and travel in carriages is not because we are haughty. We simply have no choice. You see, the price of donkeys has gone up and the *mazal* of donkeys is such that many donkeys have even become princes."

Skinny Rooster

While Reb Yehonatan was in Vienna, a prince approached him in front of a large crowd and asked the following question: "In your holy books, it is written that the Messiah will appear as a poor man riding on a donkey. You Jews are smart people; do you really believe that if the Messiah is a poor man riding a donkey, he will be able to subjugate the mighty kings and nations of the world?"

"I will answer your question in two months' time," replied Reb Yehonatan. "And in the interim, I have a request: I would like each person here to appear in two months' time with a large rooster at the king's palace."

Two months later, everyone who had been present for the question appeared at the king's palace, each with a rooster larger than the next. Reb Yehonatan also brought a rooster; however, his rooster was small and skinny.

Reb Yehonatan instructed everyone, himself included, to place their roosters in a room.

All the people watched what unfolded. The seventy roosters started to fight with each other. Reb Yehonatan's small rooster did not join the fight; it moved to the side and sat near the oven.

Eventually, all the roosters died or were gravely injured from their intense quarreling and fighting. Reb Yehonatan's rooster went over to one of the dead roosters and started eating its flesh.

Reb Yehonatan turned to the many people in attendance and said, "This is what it will look like when the Jewish Moshiach will finally appear. The nations of the world will go to war, one against the other, and they will destroy one another, and the only nation left standing will be us, the Jewish people, and our King, the Moshiach, who will then conquer the world."

A Weighty Question

On one occasion, the king was extremely angry with Reb Yehonatan, so he sent his officers to arrest him. Reb Yehonatan got wind of what was about to happen and decided to flee. Being that he was such a brilliant man, he found a hiding place that the officers were unable to discover. After a thorough search, they returned to the king empty-handed.

The king then instructed his ministers to declare that every citizen must bring their calf to the city square the next day. When they did, each calf was weighed. The ministers proclaimed that, in a month's time, each citizen must return with the same calf, and if the calf didn't weigh *exactly* the same amount, there would be serious consequences.

The citizens were extremely worried: How could they possibly ensure that their calves remained the same weight? If they fed the calf, it would gain weight, and if they didn't feed it, it would lose weight.

Reb Yehonatan saw that the elderly Jew by whom he was hiding was distraught. After hearing the king's decree, he told him not to worry; if he were to follow Reb Yehonatan's instructions, everything would be okay.

He told the elderly Jew to place the calf inside a pen, and next to the pen, he should place a bear in another enclosure. He should feed the calf as much as it wants, and with a bear in such close proximity, the calf would be very frightened and would not put on any weight.

A month later, the elderly Jew returned to the city square with his calf. Of all the calves that were weighed, the only calf that had the exact same weight was the calf of the elderly Jew.

The king's plan had worked. Only the brilliant Reb Yehonatan would be able to ensure that this calf remained the same weight. He immediately sent his officers to the home of the elderly Jew to arrest Reb Yehonatan. But when they got there, Reb Yehonatan was not to be found. He had known this whole charade was simply a means to entrap him, so as soon as the elderly Jew left home with the calf, Reb Yehonatan had fled to another excellent hiding place.

Majority Rules—Not Always

King Carlos VI had profound respect for Reb Yehonatan. On one of the many occasions they were having a philosophical discussion, the king asked Reb Yehonatan, "My esteemed rabbi, in your Torah it states that you should always follow the majority. If that is true, why don't the Jewish people convert to Christianity? There are millions more Christians in the world than there are Jews."

Having heard this question posed to him many times before, Reb Yehonatan responded, "I promise you that I will come back tomorrow to answer your question."

The next day Reb Yehonatan went running up to the gates of the king's palace, and as he tried to catch his breath, he asked the guards, "Is this the king's palace?"

They answered, "It most definitely is."

"Rabbi, why were you running?" the king asked. "You seem so confused; you know this is my palace—you have been here many times before."

"On my way here," Reb Yehonatan explained, "someone told me I was going the wrong way. I didn't pay much attention and continued walking in my usual direction. But when the man saw that I wasn't listening to him, he kept shouting that I was going the wrong way. People heard the commotion he was making, and they too started shouting at me that I was going the wrong way.

"I started running away from them, and I said to myself, *I have been to the king's palace many times before; I know where I am going, and even if a thousand people tell me I am going the wrong way, I won't listen to them.* So, my dear king, this explains why yesterday I told you I would answer your question today. We Jews know that the Torah is the truth and the word of Moshe is the truth, and even if a thousand nations say that our path is wrong and they know the true path in life, we would not listen to them. Because we know that our path will lead us to the palace of the king of the universe."

The king smiled in understanding.

Rabbi Yehonatan Eybeshitz Writes "Am Yisrael Chai" 45,760 Times to Save the Jews of Metz!

The prince of the city of Metz decreed that all the Jews of his city were to be expelled. Reb Yehonatan, the rabbi of Metz, went to see the prince. He informed the prince that no matter what he had planned, the Jewish people would live for eternity.

Upon hearing this, the prince told Reb Yehonatan, "You are known to write amulets. I will nullify my decree on condition that, within the hour, you can present an amulet no larger than the size of a mezuzah, and on it, you will write in Hebrew the statement, 'The Jewish people will live for eternity[49] 45,760 times, as there are 45,760 Jews in my city.

Reb Yehonatan returned within the hour with a square board that had 285 squares and, in each square, was another letter of the Hebrew phrase. He had placed the letter *ayin* in the middle square. He told the prince that if you read the letters in all the different directions possible, the phrase is spelled out 45,760 times.

The prince spent more than a year counting all the ways in which the phrase could be read. He was astounded to find that, indeed, the phrase appeared 45,760 times. And, as a result, the Jews were able to remain living in Metz.

Background: There are fifteen letters running horizontally and nineteen letters running vertically—in total 285 letters. The phrase Reb Yehonatan was asked to write 45,760 times contained seventeen letters.

---

49. עם ישראל חי לעולמי עד

ד	ע	י	מ	ל	ו	ע	ל	ע	ו	ל	מ	י	ע	ד
ע	י	מ	ל	ו	ע	ל	י	ל	ע	ו	ל	מ	י	ע
י	מ	ל	ו	ע	ל	י	ח	י	ל	ע	ו	ל	מ	י
מ	ל	ו	ע	ל	י	ח	ל	ח	י	ל	ע	ו	ל	מ
ל	ו	ע	ל	י	ח	ל	א	ל	ח	י	ל	ע	ו	ל
ו	ע	ל	י	ח	ל	א	ר	א	ל	ח	י	ל	ע	ו
ע	ל	י	ח	ל	א	ר	ש	ר	א	ל	ח	י	ל	ע
ל	י	ח	ל	א	ר	ש	י	ש	ר	א	ל	ח	י	ל
י	ח	ל	א	ר	ש	י	ם	י	ש	ר	א	ל	ח	י
ח	ל	א	ר	ש	י	ם	ע	ם	י	ש	ר	א	ל	ח
י	ח	ל	א	ר	ש	י	ם	י	ש	ר	א	ל	ח	י
ל	י	ח	ל	א	ר	ש	י	ש	ר	א	ל	ח	י	ל
ע	ל	י	ח	ל	א	ר	ש	ר	א	ל	ח	י	ל	ע
ו	ע	ל	י	ח	ל	א	ר	א	ל	ח	י	ל	ע	ו
ל	ו	ע	ל	י	ח	ל	א	ל	ח	י	ל	ע	ו	ל
מ	ל	ו	ע	ל	י	ח	ל	ח	י	ל	ע	ו	ל	מ
י	מ	ל	ו	ע	ל	י	ח	י	ל	ע	ו	ל	מ	י
ע	י	מ	ל	ו	ע	ל	י	ל	ע	ו	ל	מ	י	ע
ד	ע	י	מ	ל	ו	ע	ל	ע	ו	ל	מ	י	ע	ד

The phrase was spelled ayin,[50] mem,[51] yud,[52] shin,[53] reish,[54] aleph,[55] lamed,[56] chet,[57] yud,[58] lamed,[59] ayin, vov, lamed, mem, vov, ayin, and dalet.[60] The letter ayin was placed in the middle square.

In the four directions—up, down, right, and left—nine letters were written: mem, yud, shin, reish, aleph, lamed, chet, yud, and lamed.

On the next line, the letter ayin is replaced with the letter mem, and in the four directions, nine letters were written: yud, shin, reish, aleph, lamed, chet, yud, lamed, and the ninth letter is ayin.

On the next line, the letter mem is replaced with the letter yud and, in the four directions, nine letters were written: shin, reish, aleph, lamed, chet, yud lamed, ayin, and the ninth letter is vov.

This pattern continued till the last line.

Divide the 287 squares into four parts, with each part containing ten lines of eight letters.

---

50. ע
51. מ
52. י
53. ש
54. ר
55. א
56. ל
57. ח
58. י
59. ל
60. ד

ח	ל	א	ר	ש	י	ם	ע
י	ח	ל	א	ר	ש	י	ם
ל	י	ח	ל	א	ר	ש	י
ע	ל	י	ח	ל	א	ר	ש
ו	ע	ל	י	ח	ל	א	ר
ל	ו	ע	ל	י	ח	ל	א
מ	ל	ו	ע	ל	י	ח	ל
י	מ	ל	ו	ע	ל	י	ח
ע	י	מ	ל	ו	ע	ל	י
ד	ע	י	מ	ל	ו	ע	ל

If we begin with the letter *ayin* (top right corner), we can go in two directions or to the letter *mem* to the left or to the letter *mem* below.

By each letter *mem*, write the number 1, as there are two directions we can go. Next to the two letters *mem*, there are three letters *yud*.

The *yud* on the first line is connected to one letter *mem*; write the number 1 in the box.

The *yud* on the second line is connected to two letters *mem*; write the number 2 in the box.

The *yud* on the third line is connected to one letter *mem*; write the number 1 in the box.

Next to the three letters *yud*, there are four letters *shin*.

The *shin* on the first line is connected to one letter *yud*; write the number 1 in the box.

The *shin* on the second line is connected to two letters *yud*; write the number 3 (2 +1 = 3) in the box

The *shin* on the third line is connected to two letters *yud*; write the number 3 (2 +1 = 3) in the box.

The *shin* on the fourth line is connected to one letter *yud*; write the number 1 in the box.

Next to the four letters *shin*, there are five letters *resh*.

The *resh* on the first line is connected to one letter *shin*; write the number 1 in the box.

The *resh* on the second line is connected to two letters *shin*; write the number 4 (3 +1 = 4) in the box.

The *resh* on the third line is connected to two letters *shin*; write the number 6 (3 +3 = 6) in the box.

The *resh* on the fourth line is connected to two letters *shin*; write the number 4 (1 +3 = 4) in the box

The *resh* on the fifth line is connected to one letter *shin*; write the number 1 in the box.

Continuing with this process, at the bottom left corner by the letter *dalet*, there are 11,440 different ways to write the phrase. There are four sections: 11,440 × 4 = 45,760

From the *ayin* to the *mem*, there are 2 paths. From the *mem* to the *yud*, there are 4 paths. From the *yud* to the *shin*, there are 8 paths. From the *shin* to the *resh*, there are 16 paths. From *resh* to the *aleph*, there are 32 paths. From the *aleph* to the *lamed*, there are 64 paths. From the *lamed* to the *chet*, 128 paths. From the *chet* to the *yud*, 255 paths. From the *yud* to the *lamed*, 502 paths. From the *lamed* to the *ayin*, 967 paths. From the *ayin* to the *vov*, 1,804. From the *vov* to the *lamed*, 3,223. From the *lamed* to the *mem*, 5,434. From the *mem* to the *yud*, 8,437. From the *yud* to the *ayin*, 11,440.

The Chosen People

Background: On the Yom Tov of Pesach, a Jew is forbidden to possess or consume any *chametz*.

Reb Yehonatan was renowned for having a brilliant mind, but the king also considered himself a very learned individual. Therefore, from time to time, he would invite Reb Yehonatan to his palace to discuss the Jewish faith and other religions.

Reb Yehonatan had to be incredibly careful when answering the king's questions. The king could not be made to look like a fool, yet Reb Yehonatan had to ensure that the proper honor and respected were afforded to Hashem, His Torah, and the Jewish people.

On one occasion, the king asked Reb Yehonatan to explain the meaning of the biblical statement that the Jews are the chosen people. He asked, "How are Jews different from other religions and nations? If we look at the history of the Jews, we see the contrary. The Jewish people are the smallest in terms of religious groups, and they are considered inferior by all other faiths. If we are to accept the statement in the Bible as being accurate, it must be referring to the Jewish people of old."

Reb Yehonatan paused for a moment to gather his thoughts and then responded, "I believe I can demonstrate the difference between the Jewish people and people of other faiths. However, you need to promise that no harm will befall the Jewish people for what you will see today."

The king agreed.

Reb Yehonatan told the king to dress in regular clothing, and they then walked together to the synagogue. When they entered, Reb Yehonatan stood by the pulpit and declared that he has an urgent message that he needs to convey to the whole community. In a short while, the synagogue was filled to capacity.

Reb Yehonatan addressed his congregation: "By order of the king, we are prohibited from having in our possession any silk material. I want each and every one of you to go home and return with all the silk you have."

The synagogue soon emptied, and a short while later, many of the congregants had returned with silk material hidden under their coats and jackets.

Reb Yehonatan then said, "Everyone can now return home with their silk. However, you need to immediately return with the chametz you have in your homes."

The congregants looked at each other in amazement before speaking. "Reb Yehonatan, it is Pesach," said one after another. "We have no chametz in our homes. Hashem forbid we should have chametz."

"That is what I wanted to hear," Reb Yehonatan responded. He then blessed them, and they made their way out of the synagogue.

When Reb Yehonatan and the king were the only people left in the shul, Reb Yehonatan turned to the king and said, "You have officers to enforce all your laws. For instance, if someone were caught owning silk, they would be fined or imprisoned. Yet many Jews still have silk in their possession.

"On the other hand, not one of them has seen Hashem. He has no police force or army. If a Jew would transgress the word of Hashem, he would not be punished with a fine or imprisonment—yet not one of them has any chametz in their homes. The Jewish people are the chosen people, not because Hashem prefers them, but rather because we, the Jewish people, love Him unconditionally."

Moshe Spoke the Truth

When Reb Yehonatan arrived in Altona, word spread even among the non-Jewish community that the new rabbi was a man of great brilliance.

One member of the clergy approached the new rabbi and asked the following question: "The Torah relates Moshe was in heaven for forty days to receive the Torah, and during that time he did not eat or drink. How do we know that to be the truth? Was anyone with him? Perhaps prior to climbing Mount Sinai, Moshe had brought sufficient food to last forty days."

Reb Yehonatan responded, "When the Torah speaks about the birth of Moshe, the Torah specifically says that he was the child of a man and a woman. If Moshe wanted to glorify himself, he could have written that he was the son of Hashem. Furthermore, the Torah writes that Moshe's burial site remains unknown to this very day. If Moshe was seeking grandeur, he should have clearly stated where he would be buried; it would have become one of the most visited sites for the Jewish people. Clearly, Moshe always spoke the truth. Likewise, when it says that he did not eat or drink while he was in heaven receiving the Torah, he was also speaking the truth."

Seeking Revenge

Background: Yaakov had twelve sons and one daughter, Dinah. When the family was traveling to Israel, Dinah was kidnapped and raped by a man named Shechem, who was the head of his community. He decided that he wanted to marry Dinah, and he approached Dinah's brothers and suggested that the two communities join together. Her two brothers Shimon and

Levi said they would agree to the proposal under the condition that Shechem and all the men of the city undergo circumcision. They agreed, but Shimon and Levi had no intention of joining the two families. Rather, they had decided to seek revenge and wipe out all the men of the city while they were recovering from the circumcision.

An anti-Semite once stopped Reb Yehonatan on the street and asked, "Why did Shimon and Levi insist that all the men of Shechem circumcise themselves?"

Reb Yehonatan replied, "If Shimon and Levi were to wipe out a city of non-Jews, there would be a tremendous outcry from the neighboring communities. They would emphatically declare that these Jews had no right in killing so many innocent people. However, once Shechem and the others were circumcised, in the eyes of the world, they were now considered Jews. . . . And who really cares if you kill a few Jews?"

Wealth Plays No Part

Background: The manna fell from heaven for the forty years the Jews wandered in the desert. Everyone received the same amount of food regardless of how wealthy or poor a person was.

A heretic once challenged Reb Yehonatan: "In your Torah," he said, "we read that while the Jewish people were wandering in the desert, Hashem would send bread from heaven. The Jews received food without even working. Why then does the Torah write that the Jews cried?"

Reb Yehonatan responded somewhat tongue in cheek, "Human nature is that a person is most happy when he knows that he is wealthier and has more than his family and friends do. When the bread fell from heaven, everyone got the same amount. No one could boast that, while their neighbors only ate two courses, they had had a five-course meal. This made many people terribly upset—so they cried."

CHAPTER 7

TORAH LEARNING

The New Head of the Yeshiva

When Reb Yehonatan was twenty-one years old, he was appointed the maggid of Prague. One day, as the students from the yeshiva began leaving the study hall, he asked one of them what they had learned.

The student responded that they had learned a very difficult section in Rambam (Maimonides). He went on to say that the head of the yeshiva had asked a question on the Rambam, but he wasn't able to give a satisfactory answer. The head of the yeshiva had told him that he would have another opportunity to answer the question the following day.

"What was the question?" Reb Yehonatan asked.

The student shared the question, and Reb Yehonatan gave him a brilliant answer. With that, the student went on his way.

As another student walked out of the yeshiva, Reb Yehonatan asked him what they had learned that day. The conversation went similarly, and again, Reb Yehonatan answered the question. However, this time he gave a completely different answer, but the answer was just as brilliant. This happened with each of the students, and each time Reb Yehonatan gave a different answer.

חָכָם בִּיהוּדִי

הַגֶּטוֹ לִיהוּדֵי פְּרָג

The Jewish Ghetto in Prague.

The next day, when all these students gathered in the yeshiva, the head of the yeshiva repeated the question and began to discuss a possible solution. The students then started sharing with him the answers that Reb Yehonatan had given them.

"Where did you get these brilliant answers?" he asked after having heard several of them, and the students replied that the new maggid had given them the answers.

The head of the yeshiva was truly astounded. He went to see the heads of the community and informed them that this young man was worthy of being the head of the yeshiva. As a result, the head of the yeshiva of Prague removed himself, and the position was given to young Reb Yehonatan.

Cleaning House

One day, surrounded by his students, Reb Yehonatan asked them, "What does one use to clean out his house?"

The students began to debate among themselves what exactly their teacher meant, as Reb Yehonatan listened on.

One student felt that when the teacher said "house," he was referring to the human mind, and Reb Yehonatan wanted to know how much Torah does a person need to study and how many mitzvot does a person need to perform to purify one's mind?

Another student said, "No, our teacher is referring to deep mystical ideas and the house refers to the spiritual level of kingship." With that, he started to contemplate deep kabalistic ideas.

The third student suggested, "Our teacher was referring to the Bet Hamikdash, the Temple." The student then began to talk and reflect on Hashem's holy home.

Hearing all this, Reb Yehonatan chuckled. He called his wife in and asked her in front of his students, "What does one use to clean out his house?"

"A broom," she responded.

"She is right," Reb Yehonatan told his students, impressing upon them that, at times, the most obvious answer is indeed the correct one.

When to Ask a Question

Reb Yehonatan was a *rosh yeshiva* par excellence; students would travel from far and wide to attend his yeshiva. The day before class, he would inform the students of the topic he would be discussing and would give them the references and the sources on which he would be basing the class. The students would prepare for the lesson for many hours.

On one occasion, Reb Yehonatan began the class, and one of the students asked a very good question. However, Reb Yehonatan realized that the student's question showed that he had not prepared. He therefore asked another student to answer it.

Soon after, the same student posed another question. Again, Reb Yehonatan asked another student to answer.

At the end of the class, the inquisitive student was rather upset. He approached Reb Yehonatan and asked why he didn't answer the questions himself.

Reb Yehonatan explained, "If somebody had prepared for the class, he wouldn't have any questions, as all of the questions would have been answered during the preparation. A student who didn't prepare would have many questions, and time wouldn't have allowed me to answer all of them."

290 Questions

Background: Every letter of the Hebrew aleph bet has a numerical value. For example, *aleph* is one, and *yud* is ten. The Hebrew word for "fruit" is *pri*.[61] Different yeshivot have different styles of learning; for example, some styles are more analytical, while others are broader in scope.

When Reb Yehonatan was a boy, he thought a particular yeshiva led by one of the greatest rabbis of the time would be conducive to his Torah growth.

When he arrived, the head of the yeshiva was giving a class on the laws pertaining to the obligation of giving maaseh *tithe*.

The head of the yeshiva posed 290 questions, corresponding to the numerical value of the Hebrew word for *fruit*. (The reason why the head of the yeshivah specifically asked 290 questions corresponding to the numerical value of the word "fruit" was because the section of the Talmud they were studying was 'What blessing is made over fruit?'" He gave one answer that answered all 290 questions.

Reb Yehonatan was unimpressed, and he did not remain in the yeshiva. He remarked that nowhere in the Torah does it say that we need to take 290 different ideas and roll them into one for the sole purpose of demonstrating our brilliance. He said that to learn means to study the topic properly and in depth to the point at which one can pass a halachic ruling based on his studies.

---

61. פרי

Never Forget

Reb Yehonatan was once asked, "The Torah [Devorim 4:9] commands us never to forget the Torah. How is that possible? How can a person retain everything they have learned?"

Reb Yehonatan responded, "The second part of that verse gives us the answer. The posuk concludes that we are obligated in teaching our children and our students. If we teach others, we may not remember everything; however, if our students remember, it will be considered as if we remember it as well."

Oh, Is It Snowing?

On one occasion when it was snowing, Reb Yehonatan went outside to reflect on a particular section of Jewish law, and he did not return for many hours. His students became worried and went looking for him. They discovered him standing outside, covered in snow and deep in thought.

Hiding in the Cemetery

Following Reb Yehonatan's marriage, for two years, he lived in the home of his in-laws and immersed himself in the study of Torah.

A wealthy widow was the only person in the town who possessed a complete set of Talmud. He borrowed Masechta Brachot and promised to return it within a week.

However, Reb Yehonatan was inundated with halachic questions throughout the day, and he realized that he would not be able to complete the Masechta within the week as he had promised.

He therefore took the Masechta and hid in the cemetery where he knew he would not be disturbed. He was then able to complete the Masechta and return it within the week. He then borrowed the second volume, the Masechta of Shabbat, and again hid in the cemetery until he had finished learning it. And so it was with the next Masechta. . . .

Bathroom Reading Material

Background: It is prohibited to cook meat and milk together. Such food cannot be eaten or derived pleasure from. It is prohibited to think words of Torah when one is in the bathroom.

Reb Yehonatan's mind was always preoccupied with Torah thoughts. While in the bathroom, he would occupy his mind by reading secular books. One of the books described that during the winter, if you pour milk that had been with meat by the roots of a tree, the fruit will ripen quicker.

Reb Yehonatan realized that he now understood a verse in the Torah. The Torah states, "The choicest of the first fruits of your soil you shall bring to the house of the L-rd, your Hashem. You shall not cook a kid in its mother's milk."

Reb Yehonatan had struggled to comprehend the connection between the first and second parts of the verse: *What is the link between a person bringing his best fruit and the prohibition of not cooking meat and milk together?* It occurred to him that the verse is teaching us that even if you are pouring the milk that had been cooked with meat by the tree trunk to enable you to bring fruit to the Temple earlier, it is still prohibited.

Reb Yehonatan realized that reading secular works had not curtailed his mind from thinking words of Torah. On the contrary, it opened his mind to discover new understandings. He therefore decided that he would no longer read such materials in the bathroom.

A Gentle Slap

Reb Yehonatan had a world-renowned yeshiva. One of the great talmidei chachomim of the generation sent his two sons to the yeshiva to learn. Curious, this great talmid chochom-decided to pay the yeshiva a visit. When he arrived, he asked Reb Yehonatan, "How are my two sons learning?"

Reb Yehonatan responded, "One of your sons is a prodigy, and I have appointed him to be a *rosh yeshiva* to teach the other boys and help them advance in their studies. As for your other son, I had no choice but to give him a gentle slap."

The father of the boys was taken aback and asked, "Why did you slap my son?"

Reb Yehonatan told the father, "Don't be upset. Let me explain what happened: One day, as I was walking home, I overheard one of your sons giving a class to some of my students. I was enthralled by his ability; he asked brilliant questions and gave even better answers. It was a pleasure to listen to him. I decided to try to get closer without being noticed. Unfortunately, your other son saw me and told his brother to stop because I was present, so your other son immediately stopped teaching the class."

The father listened intently, and Reb Yehonatan continued to explain, "I asked him why he stopped. I told him that he should have continued, as I was sure he knew the famous Talmudic statement that a teacher is never jealous of the successes of his students. I had been enjoying myself immensely as I was listening to him teach. As such, I said to the other one, you should not have told your brother to stop giving his class. It is he to whom I gave a gentle slap."

The father was very much appeased after hearing what had taken place. He then informed Reb Yehonatan that he had another two sons who were both talmidei chachomim.

Reb Yehonatan said, "Since you have been blessed with four sons who are talmidei chachomim, after 120 years when you go to Gan Eden, you will be rewarded with a majestic chair with four legs, each leg representing one of your sons."

Passed the Test

Background: Prior to Shabbat, one is maaver the sedra. Each posuk of that week's parsha is read twice and Targum Onkelos, the Aramaic translation, once.

After serving as the chief rabbi of Metz, Reb Yehonatan was invited to become the chief rabbi of Altona, Hamburg, and Wandsbek. The previous chief rabbi of Metz (Rabbi Yaakov Yehoshua) had been appointed the chief rabbi of Frankfurt. There was a friendly rivalry between these two great centers of Jewish learning.

On his way to Altona, Reb Yehonatan spent Shabbat in Frankfurt. He was invited to address the community Shabbat afternoon. Signs were posted, informing the community of the class topic. Reb Yehonatan also listed the sources he would be referencing during the class.

The great talmidei chachomim of Frankfurt began to diligently prepare for the class; they were hoping to pose challenging questions that Reb Yehonatan would be unable to answer.

Friday afternoon, Reb Yehonatan made his way to the synagogue and began to *maaver the sedreh.*

The gabbai of the shul, who was aware what the talmidei chachomim were planning, felt pity for Reb Yehonatan. He thought, *Here he is in shul reading the Chumash when he should be at home preparing his class.* The gabbai went over to Reb Yehonatan and informed him of what would unfold the next day. Reb Yehonatan simply smiled.

The next day, the shul was filled to capacity; everyone wanted to hear the Torah thoughts of Reb Yehonatan. Reb Yehonatan's class was so profound and all-encompassing that not one of the great talmidei chachomim asked a single question or challenged him, as they had planned. At the conclusion, everyone congratulated Reb Yehonatan on his exceptional discourse.

Surrounded by a large group of listeners and with a smile on his face, Reb Yehonatan asked, "Where are all the Torah giants of Frankfurt?"

The Jews of Altona, Hamburg, and Wandsbek were extremely pleased with their rabbi and proud that he had shown the scholars of Frankfurt a glimpse into his vast knowledge and deep insights.

The Wagon Scholar

As soon as their new rabbi arrived, the heads of the community of Altona, Hamburg, and Wandsbek discussed Torah thoughts with Reb Yehonatan every chance they got. Even the wagon driver who delivered him to his new post had entered the fray and shared deep scholarly ideas!

Reb Yehonatan shared with the community leaders how amazed he was that even their wagon driver could be such a great talmid chochom. The heads of the community then informed him that the so-called wagon driver was none other than one of the great talmidei chachomim of the community. He had been so excited to meet Reb Yehonatan that he was willing to drive the wagon to ensure it would happen.

No Learning Is Learning

Background: Many people have the custom not to learn on the night preceding December 25, known as Nittel Nacht.

A bishop once asked Reb Yehonatan the following question: "It is written in your Torah that the world's existence is dependent on the Jewish people learning Torah. You have a custom of not learning Torah on the night of Nittel. How then does the world survive?"

Reb Yehonatan responded, "Our rabbis taught us that a Jewish custom is like Torah. By fulfilling the custom of not learning Torah, it is as if we are learning Torah."

Answering Questions

Reb Yehonatan writes in the *Urim V'Tumim* that when it came to answering questions, he established for himself the following rule: If the question was extremely simple, he would answer immediately. However, if it was somewhat complex, he would always look up the sources before answering the question. The reason is because our rabbis teach us that "[seeing] the words makes a person wise."

Open Book

Reb Yehonatan's custom was not to close the books he was learning from when he took a break to eat a meal; rather, he would cover the open books with a sheet out of respect.

The Truest Torah Thought

Reb Yehonatan made a *siyum* on the whole Talmud. He asked all those who were participating in the joyous occasion to share a Torah thought. He knew that some of the people sitting around the table were not great talmidei chachomim; he therefore told them that any idea they shared would be very much appreciated.

A number of men shared thoughts of Torah. The next person to rise and address everyone was a simple Jew who could barely read Hebrew. In a loud voice he said, "*Shma Yisroel Hashem Elokeinu Hashem Echod.*" And then he sat down.

Reb Yehonatan stood up and, with a broad smile, said, "These are the best words of Torah spoken." He went on to explain the reason: "All the other ideas presented, we could query and question their validity. However, this statement, that Hashem is one, is irrefutable. It is the ultimate truth."

Sacrifice Substitute

The Torah states that when a person commits an aveira, he should bring a "sin offering" to the Bes Hamikdash. When the person brought the korban, he was publicly declaring that he had transgressed the word of Hashem; this would cause him to become embarrassed and regret his actions.

The Talmud states that since we no longer have a Bes

Hamikdash, when a person studies the laws of the korbanot, it is considered the same as if he had actually brought the korban to the Temple.

Reb Yehonatan was once reflecting on the negative view people had for those who were devoting their lives to the study of Torah. Many people thought they were lazy and did not contribute to society.

Reb Yehonatan remarked, "I always wondered, *How is learning the laws of the sacrifices the same as actually bringing one?* But now I understand," he said. "When a person devotes himself to learning Torah, people make fun of him and ridicule him, and he is embarrassed. This is similar to the experience he would feel if he actually brought the korban. Therefore, learning about or bringing a korban accomplishes the same thing."

Too Stiff

While Reb Yehonatan was the rabbi of Altona, he would invite young boys to come to his house on shabbat, and he would test them on what they had learned and would reward them by giving them fruit and candy. He did this to instill in these young boys a love of Torah.

There were members in the community who didn't appreciate Reb Yehonatan's greatness and tried to embarrass him. So they found a non-Jewish boy who could speak Hebrew, and they taught him a section of Chumash.

He went on Shabbat with the other boys to be tested. The young boy started to say the Chumash. Reb Yehonatan stopped him and sent him home, declaring that the boy was not Jewish.

The people asked him how he could possibly know. He responded that when a Jewish boy learns, he naturally sways, but this boy remained as stiff as a board.

Like a Rock

Note: This is similar to the previous story; boys or men, there is no fooling Reb Yehonatan.

Two gentiles had studied the tractate Makkot and dressed themselves as religious Jews and went to be tested by Reb Yehonatan. At the conclusion of the test, Reb Yehonatan told them that they had done extremely well. However, they did not fool him. He knew they were not Jewish. When asked how he knew, Reb Yehonatan explained, "When a Jew learns, he sways, but you were both as still as a rock."

CHAPTER 8

MITZVOT

A Beautiful Sukkah and Etrog

One of Reb Yehonatan's famed students, Reb Hersh, the av
bet din of Herson, relates that, when he was studying with Reb
Yehonatan in Prague, Reb Yehonatan would adorn the walls of
his Sukkah with exquisite silk materials.[62]

On one occasion, he had purchased an etrog for the upcom-
ing festival of Sukkot. Reb Yehonatan then saw a nicer etrog, so
he purchased a second etrog. Soon after, he came across a third
etrog that was nicer still, so he purchased a third etrog.

When it came to the fulfillment of the mitzvot, Reb Yehonatan would spend a small fortune to be able to perform the mitzvah in the most beautiful manner possible.

Medicine

Background: There are 613 mitzvos. They include the prohibition
of adding to Hashem's laws or removing some of Hashem's laws.

---

62. Luchot H'Eidut, page 46

Reb Yehonatan was once asked, "What does the Talmud mean when it says the Torah is compared to an elixir of life?"

He answered, "When a doctor fills a prescription, you cannot take more of the medication; likewise, you cannot take less. Similarly, Hashem gave us 613 mitzvos. We are not permitted to invent a new mitzvah, giving us 614 mitzvos. We also cannot, on our own, reduce the number of mitzvos to 612."

No More and No Less

Note: This is a variation of the previous story.

A person once asked Reb Yehonatan, "Why does the Torah prohibit a person from adding to Hashem's mitzvos? The more commandments a person does, the better, no?"

Reb Yehonatan explained that the mitzvos could be compared to medicine. When a person is unwell, a doctor prescribes a certain amount of certain medication. If the patient takes a smaller dosage, more than likely, the medicine will not have the desired effect. Likewise, taking a larger dosage may be extremely harmful to the person's well-being.

"Hashem knows exactly how many mitzvos we need," he said. "Doing less or doing more will be harmful to our spiritual well-being."

Tzedakah (Charity)

Reb Yehonatan once approached a wealthy man for a donation. The man said that he was caring for his children and therefore had no obligation to support the rabbi's tzedokos. In support of his stance, he quoted the verse "He does tzedakah at *all times*."

(Tehillim 106:3) The Talmud (Ketubot 50b) explains the posuk as referring to a father supporting his young children.

Reb Yehonatan responded by quoting another posuk that states, "He shall not come at *all times* into the Kodesh Hakodoshim. " (Vayikra 16:3)

Background: When two posuk have a common word, rabbis may often superimpose one posuk on the other to derive homiletic lessons. The verse quoted by the wealthy man and Reb Yehonatan both had the Hebrew word *eis*,[63] which means, "all times." The verse quoted by the wealthy man is referring to tzedakah. The verse quoted by Reb Yehonatan is not referring to tzedakah. Since both posukim have the word *eis*, the verse quoted by Reb Yehonatan will be expounded to be speaking about tzedakah as well.

He explained, "When joined together by their common word, these two posukim teach us that tzedakah that is given at all times will not make a person holy, and the person will therefore not have fulfilled his obligation to give tzedakah."

Charging Interest

The Torah forbids a person to charge interest. The rabbis explain the severity of the posukim is such that a person who collects interest will not merit the resurrection of the dead.

Reb Yehonatan was once asked, "Why is the punishment so severe?"

To which he explained, "When a person charges interest, he is making money while sleeping on the job. At the time of the

---

63. עת

resurrection, we say to the person, you don't need to wake up. You can continue sleeping, and you will still be making money."

Vilna Gaon

Reb Yehonatan's student was about to embark on a lengthy trip to the city of Vilna. He had heard wonderous things about Reb Eliyahu of Vilna,[64] known as the Vilna Gaon, and had decided to study in his yeshiva. He went to his teacher for a letter of recommendation to present to the Vilna Gaon.

Reb Yehonatan took a blank piece of paper, and on the edge, he wrote two Hebrew letters: *mem* [65] and *yud*.[66] He then turned over the page and wrote the same two letters. Reb Yehonatan then folded the piece of paper and handed it to his student.

The student didn't have the audacity to ask the meaning of what Reb Yehonatan had written. The student traveled to Vilna and presented the Vilna Gaon with Reb Yehonatan's letter.

The Vilna Gaon looked at the letter and smiled. He told the student, "Your teacher wrote little, but it contained a lot."

He explained the two letters written on both sides of the page are an anacronym for the phrase stated by Akavya ben Mahalalel, who lived during the latter period of the Second Temple: "Your actions bring you close, and your actions distance you." (Ediyos 5:7)[67]

---

64. 1720–1797, a Talmudist, halakhist, Kabbalist, and the foremost leader of misnagdic (non-Hasidic) Jewry of the past few centuries.

65. מ

66. י

67. מעשיך יקרבוך ומעשיך ירחקוך - *m*aasecha *y*'karvucha u'*m*asecha *y*'rchakucha

CHAPTER 9

PRAYER

The Rest of the Day

Reb Yehonatan writes in *Yaarot Dvash* (1:5), "When I would pray Shacharit properly, it would impact my learning for the rest of the day."

With Tears

Rabbi Naftoli Hersh Washartriling, one of Reb Yehonatan's students, writes that he never met a person who mourned the destruction of the Bes Hamikdash as Reb Yehonatan did.

In every tefillah, Reb Yehonatan would shed copious tears, as he mourned its destruction and the Jewish people's lengthy exile. He would beseech Hashem to hasten the redemption and send Moshiach. This was especially true during the three weeks of mourning.

Many people were impacted by Reb Yehonatan's expression of grief and his yearning for the final redemption.

Permission to Speak

Reb Yehonatan once made the following observation: "Prior to commencing the Amidah, we beseech Hashem that He should open our mouths and allow us to speak. On the other hand, when we talk ill about another person or we slander them, we don't seek Hashem's permission. We simply talk without end."

The Lengthy Prayer

Prior to commencing the Shemoneh Esrei, we begin by beseeching Hashem as follows: *Hashem open my lips and let my mouth say your praises.*

On a regular weekday, at the conclusion of the repetition, there are a further five short prayers. On Rosh Hashanah, the repetition of the Shemoneh Esrei is extremely lengthy, as it incorporates many additional prayers that are recited by the congregation.

On Rosh Hashanah, Reb Yehonatan would pray the Shacharit at great length. He would conclude his davening prior to the reading of the Torah. Reb Yehonatan would spend a considerable amount of time on the introductory statement, *Hashem open my lips and let my mouth say your praises,* and the first blessing. He would pray with the deep and profound teachings of the great kabbalistic mystics, such as Rabbi Isaac Luria. However, during the week, his Shemoneh Esrei was not as lengthy.

Reb Yehonatan was once asked to explain why this was so. The questioner put forward his own understanding: He felt that, during the week, Reb Yehonatan was extremely involved in his learning and community affairs and perhaps that was why the Shemoneh Esrei did not take as long during the week.

"You are correct," Reb Yehonatan responded. During the week, he felt he needed to devote more time to his learning and that he was inundated with issues that he needed to resolve.

Reb Yehonatan writes that even before he arrived at the synagogue, there were matters that had been brought to his attention, and as soon as he left, he had to deal with many community affairs, which made it challenging to focus appropriately. Out of necessity, he had to shorten the amount of time spent on praying with the deep kabalistic insights. However, he also writes that he was still praying the Shemoneh Esrei when the minyan was finishing shacharis.

The Mind Is Racing

Reb Yehonatan would often speak about the importance of concentrating while davening and not to allow our minds to wander. He once explained the Talmudic statement, "Two people enter a shul to daven. One person begins to daven and doesn't wait for the other person, and when he finishes, he walks out, leaving his friend behind; his davening are of no value." (Berachot 5b)

This statement can be understood in the following manner: "Two people who enter the shul" means that a person prays with his mind and his mouth. And when the Talmud states, "One person doesn't wait for the other," this refers to the person's mind, which begins to wander to mundane matters while his mouth is still davening; such davening are of little value.

Three Steps Back

Reb Yehonatan once remarked, tongue in cheek, that when a person takes three steps back at the conclusion of the Shemonei Esreh, it would be appropriate to greet him with *sholom aleichem* and wish him *mazel tov*.

Reb Yehonatan saw that his listeners didn't quite grasp this, so he explained: "Unfortunately when a person davens, his mind wanders; his thoughts can take him to distant cities and countries. His mind can also imagine that he is taking his daughter to the chuppah. Therefore, when he takes his three steps back and comes back to reality, it would be appropriate to welcome him back and wish him mazel tov."

Moshiach

Background: In the blessing Es Tzemach Dovid, we beseech Hashem that He should send Moshiach and redeem the Jewish people.

Reb Yehonatan would often say that when one is reciting the blessing Es Tzemach Dovid in the Shemonei Esreh, he should shed tears. Because without Moshiach and the Third Bet Hamikdash in Yerushalayim, life is not worth living.

Praying Aloud

A priest once approached Reb Yehonatan with the following question: "I have noticed that you and your people pray in a very loud voice, and at times, it seems as if you are screaming. When we pray, it is done in a hushed tone. Why is this?"

Reb Yehonatan responded, "The reason is fairly obvious. Hashem is a few thousand years old. At His age, Hashem has difficulty hearing. As such, we have to say the prayers loudly. But you pray to idols that have only recently been manufactured. Because they are young, they have no problem hearing."

True Humility

Background: In the Minchah service recited on the eve of Yom Kippur and during the tefillos of Yom Kippur, we recite the Al Chet, where we list all our transgressions. At the conclusion of the list, we recite the following prayer: *Hashem, prior to my creation I wasn't worthy, during my life I am like the dust and how much more so after my passing. I am before you like a vessel full of remorse and embarrassment.*

Reb Yehonatan's minhag was to not sit in his rabbinic seat of honor during the Yom Kippur services. He preferred to sit in the back among the simple, poor folk. He explained that when he prayed in his regular place, the people around him lacked conviction. While in the back, the congregants had so much to ask Hashem for that they would pray with great devotion and shed many tears. Reb Yehonatan was hoping to be swept up by those around him.

It was the eve of Yom Kippur, and Reb Yehonatan was traveling to Altona to begin his role as chief rabbi. He came to a small town and decided to remain there over the fast. He made his way to the shul to daven Minchah. He sat next to an elderly member of the community. The elderly Jew prayed with much devotion and concentration, shedding many tears. When he came to the added section of the Al Chet, he translated each phrase into German, crying as a baby.

At the conclusion, the gabbai asked Reb Yehonatan where he would like to sit the next day. Reb Yehonatan's neighbor had davened with great fervor, so he replied that he would very much like to sit next to this elderly Jew again. He had been so moved by his davening that he was hoping to be influenced and impacted by sitting next to this man, a righteous Jew.

The next day by the reading of the Torah, the gabbai asked this elderly Jew if he would like to be called to the Torah for the fifth and final call-up. The man began berating the gabbai: How dare he offer him the final call-up?! The third and fourth call-up were *much* more prestigious. The people who had received *those* call-ups were nowhere near as important as he was! He should have been shown the proper respect and given the third or fourth call-up. He continued reprimanding the gabbai, asking him who even appointed him the gabbai. He told him to resign from his position and go home.

Reb Yehonatan could not believe what he was witnessing. This very same Jew, who had davened that he was nothing more than the dust of the earth, now had the audacity to demand a more important call-up. It wasn't as if he didn't understand the words he had been praying; he had translated every sentence into German.

At the conclusion of the service, Reb Yehonatan asked the elderly Jew if he could ask him a question. The man nodded, and he said, "I heard you daven with such introspection, declaring that you are like the dust of the earth. How could you then embarrass the gabbai and tell him how inferior he is to you and how much he needs to respect you?"

The man responded, "I don't understand your question. In my davening, I was speaking to Hashem and comparing myself to Hashem. From that view, I *am* like the dust of the earth. However, when the gabbai offered me the fifth call-up, I became extremely upset. Compared to the gabbai, I am far more superior than he will ever be."

Upon hearing this response, Reb Yehonatan exclaimed that he now understood a section of the Talmud (Yoma 89a). The Torah describes the humility of Abraham and the humility of Moshe; the humility attributed to Moshe was greater than that attributed to Abraham. Abraham compared himself to dust, and ash. Even though dirt is useless, it can still be used for something. Abraham was comparing himself to Hashem, and compared to Hashem, he was like the dust of the land.

On the other hand, Moshe described himself by saying, "What are we?" He was saying that his brother Aaron and he were like the particles that can be seen in the rays of the sun. Moshe was comparing himself to his fellow Jews. Comparing himself to other human beings in this manner is a much higher level of humility than comparing oneself to Hashem.

Shul Honors

Reb Yehonatan was extremely upset about a certain aspect of shul life. He felt that, in the shul, all people were equal and that favoritism should not be shown to one member over the other.

Though he wrote that the community of Metz did not have this problem, he pointed out that in some shuls, the infighting over who should be honored in leading the minyan, called to the

Torah, or blowing the shofar resulted in matters being brought before secular court. He suggested that lots should be drawn to allocate the various honors bestowed during the service.

Aleinu

Background: The last section of shacharis is the Aleinu prayer. Depending on its context, a Hebrew word can have more than one meaning. The word *Aleinu* in this prayer means, "upon us."

When Reb Yehonatan was chief rabbi of Metz, the RaM-CHaL[68] once came to the city for a visit. He would come every morning to the shul to daven. However, he always came at the conclusion of the davening when the minyan had finished reciting Aleinu daven.

The RaMCHaL explained that since he davened based on the *kavonos* (Kabalistic insights) of the Arizal,[69] it took him a long time to daven, and he didn't want the minyan to wait for him.

Reb Yehonatan explained the RaMCHaL's behavior by quoting the posuk, "A holy man of Hashem passes by us regularly." (Melachim II 4:9)

Background: The posuk is referencing a prominent woman telling her husband that there is a holy man that passes by us regularly. In this posuk, the Hebrew word for "passes by us" is *over aleinu*. By using the word *aleinu* in the posuk, it can be alluding to the Aleinu prayer.

---

68. Rabbi Moshe Chaim Luzzatto (1707–1746), a prominent Italian Kabbalist and philosopher.

69. Rabbi Isaac Luria (1534–1572), considered the father of contemporary Kabbalah.

Reb Yehonatan was inferring that the holy man, the RaM-CHaL, would come to pray "after the final prayer—the Aleinu—had passed."

Children versus Servants

A bishop once asked Reb Yehonatan, "Why is it that whenever I walk past the shul, there is always so much noise and people talking, while when you pass our places of worship, you can hear a pin drop?"

Having heard this question more than once, Reb Yehonatan answered, "We see ourselves as Hashem's children, and children always make noise when they are at home. You consider yourselves as Hashem's servant, and servants must always show reverence and decorum."

Healing the Sick

A bishop once approached Reb Yehonatan with the following question: "In your daily prayers, you bless Hashem for healing the Jew who is ill. Does Hashem only heal the Jew? Who then heals the other nations?"

Reb Yehonatan explained, "This is the eighth bracha of the Shemonei Esreh, and it alludes to the mitzvah of bris milah where we are commanded to circumcise every male child on the eighth day. Since the obligation of bris milah applies only to the Jewish people, the bracha specifically mentions the Jew."

The bishop was satisfied with this response. However, Reb Yehonatan's students had overheard the discussion and asked him if this was the correct answer.

Reb Yehonatan replied, "No, it is not. This is evident from the bracha we recite in the morning and every time we go to the bathroom, where we thank Hashem for healing all of mankind. Hashem created the laws of nature. They include the ability for a person who has become ill to be cured. When we say the Shemonei Esreh and make specific reference to Hashem healing the Jewish people, we are thanking Hashem that we can be healed even beyond the laws of nature."

Praying for the Sick

Reb Yehonatan would often say, "When one davens for the sick, one should have in mind all the Jewish people who are unwell. A person shouldn't think, *Since I don't know them or we are not related, why pray for them?* We need to view every Jew as if they are our brother or child. A person needs to understand that the Jewish people are like one soul and one body, and when one Jew is unwell, it as if one of the limbs or organs of all Jewish people need healing."

CHAPTER 10

Interaction with Community

Beloved

Reb Yehonatan was so beloved by his community that many would have a painting of his regal appearance hanging in their homes. Some would hug and kiss the painting. Many named their sons Yehonatan as a sign of their love and respect for their beloved rabbi.

Rabbi of Metz

Background: During the tefilos of the Yomim Noroim, there are many tefilos in which the chazan recites a verse and the minyan repeats the same verse. One such tefilah is called Melech Elyon, the King Above, which refers to the King of Kings.

Prior to being offered the position as rabbi of Metz, Reb Yehonatan spent Rosh Hashanah with the community. The minhag of the community was for the rabbi to lead the minyan in the recital of the tefilah Melech Elyon. As they had not yet appointed a rabbi to fill the position, they asked Reb Yehonatan to lead the tefilah.

Reb Yehonatan remarked, "Rather than the congregation of Metz asking me to lead the tefilah Melech Elyon, I would prefer if the Melech Elyon [Hashem] would ask me to become the rabbi of Metz."

Over a Barrel of Wine

Reb Yehonatan was sitting in his study when a very distraught person walked in. The man explained that he was a wagon driver who made his living transporting goods for people. On his latest trip, he was carrying barrels of wine and had hidden all his money under one of the barrels. When he arrived, his money was missing.

"It must have been stolen," he lamented. "I don't know what to do."

Reb Yehonatan asked, "Who else was in the carriage?"

The wagon driver said, "The owner of the wine and his non-Jewish worker."

Reb Yehonatan instructed the driver to bring the Jewish owner. When he arrived, Reb Yehonatan asked him directly if he had stolen the driver's money. The owner became extremely defensive, accusing Reb Yehonatan of proclaiming an innocent man guilty. He then turned to the wagon driver and berated him for even suspecting that he would have taken the Jew's hard-earned money.

Reb Yehonatan then asked if the owner of the wine if he had seen the non-Jewish worker take the money, to which he replied that he did not.

Background: In times of old, wine was used as part of idolatry practice. The Torah prohibited such wines. The rabbis instituted that kosher wines must only be handled or moved by a Jew. If the non-Jew had taken the money, he would have needed to move the barrels, and as a result, the wine would be rendered non-kosher.

After thinking awhile, Reb Yehonatan said he was ready to give his decision based on the following line of reasoning: He believed the wagon driver had placed his money under one of the barrels. He also believed that the Jewish wine owner did not take the money. Therefore, the only remaining suspect was the non-Jewish worker. And since the non-Jew had taken the money, it meant that he had moved the barrels of wine to do so. That being the case, all the wine was now prohibited.

When the wine owner heard this, he broke down in tears. He confessed that he had, in fact, stolen the money and would now return it to its rightful owner.

Lacking in Gratitude

Reb Yehonatan was the rabbi of a small community. He was extremely devoted to his congregation, caring for all their needs—big and small. He established a soup kitchen for the needy and distributed *tzedakah* to the poor.

One day, a large and respectable delegation from the city of Prague came to see him. They had in their possession a letter of appointment. The Prague community wanted to appoint Reb Yehonatan as a rabbi of the Prague community. All the rabbis of Prague had signed the contract.

Reb Yehonatan requested that the heads of his community

come immediately to his home. When they arrived, he asked them to read the letter of appointment from the Jewish community of Prague. After reading the letter, they returned it to Reb Yehonatan.

Though he said nothing, Reb Yehonatan grew angry and embarrassed. He could not understand why the heads of his community had remained silent after reading the letter. After all he had done for the community, he would think that they would protest and demand that their rabbi not leave. What would the delegation of Prague think of him that no one even uttered a word?

News spread among his congregation that he would soon be moving to the city of Prague. The community as well didn't protest or beseech the rabbi to remain.

Several days prior to Reb Yehonatan's departure, he asked that all the members of the congregation gather in the shul, as he wished to address them one last time. Reb Yehonatan rose to the pulpit, and in a very harsh tone and strong language, he chastised and rebuked his community. He spoke strongly of the importance of fulfilling Hashem's mitzvos.

Reb Yehonatan felt that his community was lacking in the important quality of expressing gratitude. He believed that after all he had done for his community, they should have at least voiced their desire that he should remain. Their silence was deafening, and therefore, he thought he had no choice but to reprimand them.

A Question of Time

Reb Yehonatan was appointed a rabbi of Prague when he was only eighteen years old. He became aware that there were those who were unhappy that they had appointed such a young man to be their rabbi. Rabbi Yehonatan asked that the following message be relayed to them: "You should not be overly concerned; if it is a problem, it will pass with the passage of time."

First off the Rank

Reb Yehonatan was attending the funeral of one of his contemporaries. The eulogies were about to commence when an uncouth, ignorant Jew, a former student of the deceased, pushed his way through the crowd until he stood next to the coffin and began to say a eulogy.

Everyone started to yell at him to stop speaking. Reb Yehonatan, on the other hand, seemed to believe this man *should* be the first speaker.

When asked to explain, Reb Yehonatan said the following: "Our rabbis contrast what happens when a Torah scholar ages with what happens when an unlearned person ages. The older a simple person gets, the sillier and more ignorant he becomes. However, when a talmid chochom ages, he becomes wiser. [Kinnim 3:6] It makes sense to let the fool speak first, because the later he speaks, the more ridiculous and absurd his speech will be. Meanwhile, the later the talmid chochom speaks, the wiser his words will be."

The Shabbat Hagadol Speech

Background: A) The Shabbat before Pesach is called Shabbat Hagadol, and it is customary for the rabbi to deliver a lengthy discourse to the whole congregation. B) The custom is to read from the Haggadah in preparation for the seder. C) When reading from the Torah, it must be read in a sing-song fashion. D) Each word has a particular note attached to it. Each note has a name that it is called by. E) Each letter of the aleph bet has a numerical value.

One year on Shabbat Hagadol, Reb Yehonatan made his way to the bimah, which was in the center of the shul to begin his yearly address. As he was walking up the steps, he noticed a non-scholarly Jew walking behind him. The congregation was bewildered: What was this man doing, walking on to the bimah as Reb Yehonatan was about to deliver his scholarly address?

This simple man turned to Reb Yehonatan and said, "My esteemed and beloved rabbi, could I possibly ask you a question?"

With the utmost humility, Reb Yehonatan replied, "Of course you can, and I will do my best to try to answer what is on your mind."

"Today, I read part of the Haggadah, and I came to a section I could not understand. The Haggadah quotes a verse of the Torah that reads, 'The Egyptians made the lives of the Jews extremely bitter.' And I noticed that the notes on the words, 'The Egyptians made the lives of the Jews extremely bitter' is *kadmo v'azlo*—these are notes of happiness and joy. How can we say the words, 'The Egyptians made the lives of the Jews extremely bitter' in a happy tone?"

Reb Yehonatan, in a resounding voice, said, "My dear son, you have asked a *brilliant* question. Let me answer it: You know that Hashem told Abraham that we would be in Mitzrayim for 400 years. If so, why were we only there for 210 years?"

בֶּחָכָם בִּיהוּדִי

(שֶׁהִקְדִּימוּ לָצֵאת מִמִּצְרַיִם) לִפְנֵי הַמּוֹעֵד בְּמֵאָה
וְתִשְׁעִים שָׁנָה, כְּמִנְיַן קַדְמָא וְאַזְלָא, וְזוֹהִי סִבַּת
הַשִּׂמְחָה, וְזֶהוּ אַף הַטַּעַם לְכָךְ, שֶׁמְּלִים אֵלּוּ
הִטְעֲמוּ דַּוְקָא בְּקַדְמָא וְאַזְלָא!״

הִשְׁתּוֹמְמוּ הַנֶּאֱסָפִים לְמִשְׁמַע דִּבְרֵי
הַחֲרִיפוּת שֶׁל רַבָּם הַגָּדוֹל, וַהֲנָאָתָם גָּדְלָה עַד
לִמְאֹד.

He paused for a moment and then continued, "There are many reasons given. One of them is that the slavery and brutality we experienced in only 210 years would have normally been experienced over a period of 400 years. Therefore, Hashem redeemed us early, as we had, in a sense, lived through 400 years of slavery. That is why the musical notes on the words, 'The Mitzriyim made the lives of the Jews extremely bitter' are happy notes. It was because of how the Mitzrayim treated us that we were able to leave Mitzrayim 190 years earlier."

In his true brilliance, Reb Yehonatan did not stop there. He asked the congregation, "There are many notes that impart a joyful melody. Why then does the Torah specifically use the notes *kadmo v'azlo*?" Reb Yehonatan then provided the answer: "The words *kadmo v'azlo* have a numerical value of 190. The *kuf* is 100, the *dalet* is 4, the *mem* is 40, the *aleph* is 1, the *vov* is 6, the *aleph* is 1, the *zayin* is 7, the *lamed* is 30, and the *aleph* is 1.

"The Jews were meant to be in Mitzrayim for 400 years; they were there for only 210 years. They left 190 years earlier than the designated time. If you minus 210 from 400, you are left with 190, which is the numerical value of the words *kadmo v'azlo*. Furthermore, the translation of the words *kadmo v'azlo* means to go prior to the designated time. The Torah specifically chose these two cantorial notes since its translation and numerical value clearly reflect the exodus from Mitzrayim."

The congregation was in awe of Reb Yehonatan's profound and brilliant idea, delivered without *any* preparation.

Porcelain Ornaments

After Reb Yehonatan arrived in Altona, he addressed the community and chastised them for having porcelain ornaments from India proudly displayed in their homes. He felt that it was inappropriate, as perhaps the ornaments had been made for the purpose of idol worship. He therefore instructed his community to destroy them. Reb Yehonatan was held in such esteem that his instruction was adhered to by every member of the congregation.

The Butcher

Reb Yehonatan was once asked to explain the following:

Why, if a butcher goes to a rabbi with a question about whether an animal is kosher, and the rabbi decides that it is not kosher, the butcher accepts the decision without any qualms, even though there may be a great financial loss—but if the butcher has a disagreement with another person and they go to the rabbi to adjudicate and he passes judgment in favor of the other person, more often than not, the butcher will become angry with the rabbi, even though the loss is much less than when he approached the rabbi concerning the kashrut of the animal?

Reb Yehonatan explained, "When the rabbi said the animal is not kosher, only the butcher loses. However, in the case of a dispute with another person, the butcher is not upset that he *lost* money; he is upset that someone else *made* money."

Back to Front

Reb Yehonatan once remarked, "The rabbis state that when a judge sits in judgment prior to giving his decision, he should view both litigants as being guilty. Once the decision has been given and the parties have carried out the decision, the judge should view both parties as being righteous." (Avot 1:8)

"Unfortunately," he added, "this is not the case from the perspective of the litigants. Prior to the judge rendering his decision, the litigants view the judge as being righteous and honest. Once the decision has been given, more often than not, one of the parties and sometimes both parties are unhappy and disgruntled with the ruling. The parties no longer hold the judge in high esteem."

The Holy Groom

Background: A) The custom is for a kallah and chatan not to see each other for a week leading up to their wedding. B) On Simchat Torah, we conclude the reading of the Torah. The person who is called for the final section is known as Chatan Torah, the groom of the Torah. And the Torah is called the Kallah, the bride. Many shuls have the minhag of selling this honor. Traditionally, it is given to the rabbi who is the greatest talmid chacham in the community.

One year on Simchat Torah in Reb Yehonatan's shul, a very wealthy Jew bought Chatan Torah and honored himself with the call-up. Reb Yehonatan, who was not amused remarked, "Our Chatan is very religious—he hasn't seen his Kallah for a whole year."

Talk to One Another

Reb Yehonatan once lamented that at the root of most conflicts is the inability or desire to talk. If people would only talk to one another and share their concerns and gripes, they may come to the realization that their disagreement has absolutely no substance.

What a Fool

A person came to Reb Yehonatan seeking advice on how to repent for all his many sins. However, he was too embarrassed to tell Reb Yehonatan that he was the sinner. He therefore said that his friend had sent him, and he listed a litany of aveiros for which his "friend" wished to repent. When he concluded, Reb Yehonatan said, "The person who sent you here is a fool. The sinner could have come to me himself and told me that he was asking on behalf of a friend."

A New Haggadah

Reb Yehonatan was once asked, "Why is it that every year Haggadot with new commentary are published. Why can't we simply use the ones from last year?"

Reb Yehonatan responded, "Every year, the spiritual level of the Jewish people decreases and last year's *rasha* is this year's *tzaddik*. We need to print new Haggadot suitable for this year's *rasha*."

Election of Leaders

Reb Yehonatan once remarked, "Moshe was the greatest leader of the Jewish people. He led the Jewish people out of Mitzrayim, and he ascended Mount Sinai to receive the Torah. Yet Moshe recognized that it would not be advantageous for him to self-appoint men to positions of leadership. He therefore instituted that elections should be held to appoint the leaders of the tribes. A leader needs to realize that he has been appointed by the people and therefore he is duty bound to report back to them."

Bris Milah

An enlightened Jew refused to circumcise his son. He explained that non-Jewish scholars had proven that bris milah was, in fact, an ancient Egyptian practice copied by the Jews and other nations.

Reb Yehonatan responded that it seems the enlightened Jew places great weight on the opinions expressed by non-Jewish scholars. While it is true the Mitzrayim circumcised themselves, that was a result of Yoseph, the viceroy of Mitzrayim, insisting they do so.

The Jew could not accept Reb Yehonatan's understanding of events and claimed it made absolutely no sense for Yoseph to insist that the Mitzrayim be circumcised. What could Yoseph gain by insisting everyone gets circumcised?

Reb Yehonatan answered, "Yoseph knew that there would be Jews who follow any custom of the non-Jews, even if they make no sense, and will listen to anything their scholars will say. Insisting the Mitzrayim be circumcised would encourage non-believing Jews to circumcise their sons."

A Cold Donkey

Even though it was midsummer, the day was unusually cold, so Reb Yehonatan walked to shul wearing his winter coat.

A passerby in his summer clothing whose teeth were chattering saw Reb Yehonatan and wanted to make fun of him. He shouted, "Rabbi, our Talmud says that donkeys feel the cold even during the summer!" The passerby was inferring that since Reb Yehonatan was wearing a winter coat during the summer, he must be a donkey.

Reb Yehonatan responded, "You misunderstood the Talmudic statement you just quoted. Do you know what the definition of a *fool* is?"

The teeth-chattering man grew redder in the face. He knew the question was rhetorical.

Reb Yehonatan continued, "A fool is someone who is embarrassed to dress warmly on a cold day during the summer months and would rather walk around freezing. The Talmudic statement, 'a donkey feels the cold in the summer' should not be taken at face value to mean that a donkey is always cold, even in the hot summer months. Rather, the word *donkey* is referring to a human who is acting like a donkey. You . . ." said Reb Yehonatan, "are the donkey that feels the cold in the summer because you are foolish enough to wear summer clothes even though it is very cold outside. A smart person, on the other hand, wakes up on a cold morning in the middle of the summer and puts on his coat to stay warm."

בֶּחָכָם בִּיהוּדִי

חֲמוֹר) קַר לוֹ בִּתְקוּפַת תַּמּוּז — — — — אַף לֹא
כֵן מִנְהָגוֹ שֶׁל הֶחָכָם: הֶחָכָם לֹא יֵבוֹשׁ לְהִתְלַבֵּשׁ
אַף בִּמְעִיל פַּרְוָה, כַּאֲשֶׁר קַר בַּחוּץ — וִיהֵא זֶה
אֲפִלוּ בְּחֹדֶשׁ תַּמּוּז — וַאֲזַי יֵחַם לוֹ...״

* שַׁבָּת כ״ג, ע״א

172

CHAPTER 11

CONFLICT WITH RABBI YAAKOV EMDEN

Who Is Greater?

After Reb Yehonatan served as rabbi of Prague, he accepted the position as the head of the bet din and the yeshiva in the city of Metz. He succeeded Rabbi Yaakov Yehoshua Falk, who had been appointed chief rabbi of Frankfurt.

An argument broke out between the students of Rabbi Yaakov Yehoshua and Reb Yehonatan. Rabbi Yaakov's students felt that while Reb Yehonatan was a great Talmudist, he was not on par with their rabbi when it came to halachic rulings. Reb Yehonatan's students felt while Rabbi Yaakov was a great halachic decider, he was not of the caliber as Reb Yehonatan when it came to Talmudist greatness.

Tradition has it that as a result, both rabbis wrote monumental works in the area the students felt they were lacking. Rabbi Yaakov Yehoshua wrote the *Pnei Yehoshua*, which is a commentary on the Talmud, and Reb Yehonatan wrote the *Kreiti U'Pleti* and the *Urim V'Tumim* on the Shulchan Aruch.

Rabbis Are Peacemakers

Background: The Talmud states that the rabbis bring peace to the world.

Reb Yehonatan had a lot of opposition while he was rabbi in Altona. He once remarked, "There are times when two people who are sworn enemies will unite against a common foe. People who may hate one another will put their own personal feud aside and unite in their opposition of the rabbi."

In jest, he said, "The Talmud sings the praise of the rabbis that they bring peace to the world. This is true because the rabbis are causing enemies to come together in their common goal of causing strife to their rabbi."

Mind Your Own Business

Background: At the conclusion of the seder on the night of Pesach, the custom is to sing a song called "Chad Gadya" (one kid). It speaks about a chain of events that begin with a cat attacking a kid and culminates in Hashem's intervention.

One of the great disagreements that engulfed the Jewish world was the dispute between Reb Yehonatan and Reb Yaakov Emden. On one occasion, Reb Yehonatan was sitting in an inn, and at the adjoining table was a group of Jews discussing the dispute. They were unaware that Reb Yehonatan was sitting at the very next table.

Reb Yehonatan approached them and asked if he could ask them a question. They answered in the affirmative. He said, "In the Chad Gadya, the cat is at fault because it attacks the kid. The dog was right to attack the cat because it was defending the goat. The stick that hit the dog is at fault. The fire that burnt the stick is fine. The water that extinguished the fire is at fault. The ox that drank the water is fine. The slaughterer that slaughtered the ox is at fault. The angel of death that killed the slaughterer is fine. Hashem who punished the angel of death is at fault. How is it possible that Hashem could be considered at fault?"

They had no answer.

Reb Yehonatan explained: "Why did the dog get involved? Why didn't it mind its own business? Perhaps the kid had done something wrong that the dog didn't see? The dog is therefore wicked. The stick is fine, and the fire is wicked. The water is fine, and the ox is wicked. The shochet is fine and the angel of death is wicked, and Hashem is therefore in the right. Who asked the dog to get involved? Let the dog mind its own business. Likewise . . ." Reb Yehonatan continued, "why are you discussing the dispute between Reb Yehonatan Eybeshitz and Reb Yaakov Emden when you know nothing about the conflict? You are simply fanning the fires of the dispute."

Sticks and Stones

During the height of the conflict between Reb Yehonatan and Reb Yaakov Emden, Reb Yehonatan was told that his opponents were planning to attack him with sticks and stones. Reb Yehonatan laughed and said that he was not afraid of a physical confrontation. And he cited the Torah story of the twelves spies as the reason this was so.

"Before the spies left for the Land of Israel, Moshe prayed to Hashem that He should protect Yehoshua from the recommendation of the other spies. When the spies returned, only two of the spies—Yehoshua and Calev—brought back a positive report. The Torah relates that the Jewish people wanted to stone Yehoshua and Calev."

Reb Yehonatan then raised the following: "Moshe prayed to Hashem that he should be safeguarded against the opinion of the spies; why didn't he subsequently daven that he should be protected from physical assault? From this we learn that we need to be more concerned what our fellow Jew says about us than what they want to do to us physically."

No Blood Flow

Background: A) In Talmudic language, a murderer is called a *shofchei domim*, a spiller of blood. Jewish law equates someone who embarrasses another person or promulgates controversy with a *shofchei domim*. B) Korach was a relative of Moshe from the tribe of the Levites who started a revolt against Moshe. He felt that Moshe had taken all the positions of authority and leadership for himself and his brother Aaron. C) The Torah lists the lineage of Korach up to but not including Yaakov.

Reb Yehonatan once lamented to his students that his conflict with Reb Yaakov Emden had taken a bitter toll on his life—to the extent that if they were to cut his skin, his blood wouldn't flow.

Reb Yehonatan said that he found solace in the fact that far greater individuals had to combat and deal with opposition when they were attacked with frivolous unsubstantiated claims. And who greater than Moshe, who was attacked by Korach?

When the Torah lists the lineage of Korach, it does not mention that he was a descendant of Yaakov as Yaakov requested that his name not be mentioned in connection with a dispute.

Reb Yehonatan contrasted our forefather Yaakov, who shunned conflict, and another Yaakov, Rabbi Yaakov Emden, who had instigated their dispute.

Hashem Is Eternal

Aa a renowned Kabbalist, Reb Yehonatan would often write amulets for those in need. This led to the great conflict between Reb Yehonatan and Reb Yaakov Emden, who believed that Reb Yehonatan's amulets proved that he was a follower of Shabbtai Tzvi, the false messiah.

Certain individuals went to the authorities with trumped-up charges against Reb Yehonatan. They said he was planting seeds of dissention against the king and the clergy. As a result, Reb Yehonatan was placed under arrest.

On a daily basis, representatives of the king and the priests came to question him. They wanted him to bring proof from his Torah to the authenticity of his faith and that he was truly an upright person who would not denigrate the king. They told him they would accept even a subtle proof, and it did not need to be something written black on white. And, if he couldn't, he would have to convert or be put to death.

Reb Yehonatan requested that he be given three days to prepare. For the next three days, he fasted and prayed. He asked Hashem to guide him to answer their questions. On the third day, the delegation returned, and they saw Reb Yehonatan wearing his *tallit* and *tefillin* and studying.

They asked what book he was reading. He answered that he was reading the third book of the Torah called Vayikra. He read the posuk he was studying: "You shall not make idols for yourselves, nor shall you set up a statue or a monument for yourselves." (Vayikra 26:1)

They responded that they too believed in Hashem and did not practice idol worship. Reb Yehonatan then told them that he was also studying the section of Bechukotai (the last section of Vayikra). The section begins with the words, "If [you will follow] My statutes."[70]

The first word has two letters: an *aleph*[71] and a *mem.*[72] Those two letters are the first letters of the following words when written in Hebrew:

- The nations ask[73]
- Where is your Hashem[74]
- We answer[75]
- Our Hashem is King[76]

The second word is "statutes."[77] It is comprised of five Hebrew letters. Using each Hebrew letter to commence a new word, we get the following phrase, "In heaven[78] [Hashem] is alive[79] [He] exists and [He] rules forever."

Reb Yehonatan told them that this proves Hashem is eternal. The delegation was so impressed by his brilliance and by his holy countenance that they freed him and removed all baseless charges against him.

---

70. אם בחוקותי

71. א

72. When written in the middle of a word it is written מ and at the end of a word it is written ם

73. אומות מקשין

74. אייה מלככם

75. אנו משיבים

76. אלקינו מלך

77. בחקתי

78. בשמים

79. חי

No Rest

During the height of the conflict between Reb Yehonatan and Reb Yaakov, one of Reb Yehonatan's students spoke disparagingly about his own teacher. When Reb Yehonatan was informed, he was extremely upset with him. Reb Yehonatan said that his student would have no rest. He would constantly be moving from one place to another, never being able to call one place home.

The student lived like a wayfarer, always on the move. Eventually he arrived on the eve of Shabbat in Kushta, Turkey. He made his way to the local synagogue where the rabbi was a great Torah figure—Chacham Yitzchak Bachar David. The minhag was that at the end of the Friday night davening, all the guests would remain in the shul, and the rabbi would direct the guests to the homes of their hosts. The rabbi allocated all the guests but not Reb Yehonatan's student.

The next day after the morning service, once again the rabbi told each guest where they would be eating Shabbat lunch. Everyone but the student had a place.

In the afternoon, the rabbi arrived at the shul to give a shiur. The student asked the rabbi a question, but the rabbi refused to answer him. He asked a second and then a third question, and each time, the rabbi refused to answer.

The student became very upset and began to cry. He said to the rabbi, "You didn't give me a place to eat, and you don't answer my questions. What have I done so terribly wrong?"

The rabbi responded, "It seems a great rabbi is upset with you."

The student couldn't recall what he had done wrong. He then remembered the episode with Reb Yehonatan. He told the rabbi that he would immediately travel to Prague to ask Reb Yehonatan for forgiveness.

The rabbi responded, "I am not sure you will find him."

Unsure what the rabbi meant, the student left and traveled to Prague. When he arrived at Reb Yehonatan's shul, Reb Yehonatan's coffin was being carried to the cemetery.

The student now understood what the rabbi had meant.

The Amulet Crisis

One of the most tragic episodes in Reb Yehonatan's life that impacted world Jewry was the fiery argument between Reb Yehonatan and Reb Yaakov Emden, the son of the Chacham Tzvi.

Reb Yaakov, who lived in Altona, falsely suspected Reb Yehonatan of being part of the messianic cult led by Shabbtai Tzvi. He reached this conclusion partly due to various amulets supposedly written by Reb Yehonatan that contained alleged heretical writings.

At the time, one of the great leaders of the Jewish world was Rabbi Eliyahu of Vilna. He wrote that Reb Yehonatan was one of the great leaders of the times, a great Torah scholar who was proficient in all areas of the Torah and had deep understanding.

"And I have seen the amulets penned by Reb Yehonatan," he stated, "and they are all authentic and have been written while drawing from great spiritual heights." He concludes by saying, "I am in pain since the Sefer Torah [Reb Yehonatan] is in pain."

CHAPTER 12

FINAL DAYS

The Last Stop

Background: Reb Yehonatan's final rabbinic position was chief rabbi of three united communities AHU (Altona, Hamburg, and Wandsbek). In Hebrew, the three cities were referred to by the first letter of each city, *aleph*,[80] *hey*,[81] and *vov*.[82] The word "desire" in Hebrew is spelled *aleph, hey,* and *vov*—the same three letters that represent Reb Yehonatan's rabbinical position.

When Reb Yehonatan came to take up the position as rabbi of the three communities, he saw the beautiful house that had been prepared, and he remarked by quoting the posuk, "He desired it for His habitation. This is my resting place forever; here I shall dwell for I desired it." (Tehillim 132:14–15)

Reb Yehonatan quoted this verse because it alluded to his new rabbinic position. Indeed, this was the final rabbinic post Reb Yehonatan held prior to his passing.

---

80. א

81. ה

82. ו

Carried

During Reb Yehonatan's final illness, the community spared no expense in bringing the top doctors to treat their beloved rabbi. When Reb Yehonatan was too weak to walk to shul, his congregants carried him there in a chair or a bed.

On His Deathbed

Reb Yehonatan was deathly ill. It seemed he had little time still to live. The heads of the Altona community came to pay their final respect. They leaned close to Reb Yehonatan and asked him who he thought was suitable to assume his position after his passing.

In a very soft, barely audible voice, he whispered, "Perhaps Rebi Meir."

After Reb Yehonatan's passing, the elders began searching for the great Torah scholar Rebi Meir, who would be fitting to fill the shoes of their beloved rabbi. Try as they may, they could not find a rabbi of such stature by the name of Rebi Meir.

They decided that this would be the question they would pose to all prospective candidates. The candidate who could explain Reb Yehonatan's answer would be worthy to be his successor.

Rabbi Yitzchak Halevi Horowitz, who was the chief rabbi of Brody, came to be interviewed and was asked to explain what Reb Yehonatan meant.

He explained that Reb Yehonatan was not referring to a particular rabbi who should be his replacement. Rather, he was referring to the great sage Rebi Meir, who is mentioned in the Mishnah. The Talmud states that most individuals who are in the final stages of dying will, in fact, pass away. And there are certain halachic rulings based on this principle. Rebi Meir disagreed with this principle; he was of the opinion that we must always consider the slim possibility that the dying person will recover.

Reb Yitzchak explained, "When you asked Reb Yehonatan who should succeed him, he was saying that maybe the opinion of Rebi Meir is correct, and I may possibly recover and there will be no need to appoint a new rabbi."

The Maidservant

Background: Righteous Jews say Tikun Chaizot, a special prayer lamenting the destruction of the Bet Hamikdash at midnight.

After Reb Yehonatan's passing, his students asked the maidservant if she could please share some of her memories. She said two things come to mind: "The first, the rabbi never once looked in my direction, and second, every night at midnight, the rabbi would begin to cry and wail as if it was his last day on earth."

The Dream

Tradition has it that some time after Reb Yehonatan's passing, he returned in a dream to one of the leading rabbis of the generation and told him the following. Reb Yaakov Emden and myself—we are in Gan Eden[83] while the people who fueled the fire of our disagreement are in Gehenom.[84]

---

83. Garden of Eden
84. Hell

הֶחָכָם בִּיהוּדִי

בְּשׁוּרוֹת שֶׁכָּתַב בָּא לִידֵי בִּטּוּי כְּאֵבוֹ הַגָּדוֹל עַל הָרְדִיפוֹת וְהָעֶלְבּוֹנוֹת שֶׁסָּפַג בִּימֵי חַיָּיו עֲלֵי אֲדָמוֹת, וַעֲצָתוֹ לְכָל אָדָם לִבְרֹחַ מִן הַגְּדֻלָּה וְהָרַבָּנוּת:

יִרְאוּ כָּל עוֹבֵר הֶחָרוּת עַל הַלּוּחוֹת

הָאִישׁ אֲשֶׁר עָמַד לְנֵס וְהָיָה כְּשׁוּשָׁן פּוֹרַחַת

וְשָׁב אֶל עָפָר וּמַרְאֵהוּ מֵאִישׁ נִשְׁחָת

נָא שִׂימוּ עַל לְבַבְכֶם וְשׁוּבוּ בִּתְשׁוּבָה נוֹצַחַת

תְּפִלָּה תַּרְבּוּ בַּעֲדוֹ לֵאלֹקֵי הָרוּחוֹת

נַפְשׁוֹ אֵלָיו יֵאָסֵף וּבַל תִּהְיֶה נִדַּחַת

זְכוּת מַעֲשֵׂיכֶם יָגֵנּוּ כִּי נַפְשׁוֹת יִשְׂרָאֵל אַחַת

לִמְדוּ מוּסָר לְשֹׁנָא כָּבוֹד וּמִגְדֻלָּה

תִּהְיֶה נַפְשְׁכֶם בּוֹרַחַת

דְּמוּתוֹ שֶׁל "הֶחָכָם הַיְּהוּדִי", הָעֲטוּרָה כֶּתֶר תּוֹרָה וְכֶתֶר מַלְכוּת וְהַמַּזְכִּירָה לָנוּ אֶת כָּל הַחָכְמָה וְאֶת כָּל הַחֵן שֶׁל הַיַּהֲדוּת, נִשְׁאֲרָה חֲקוּקָה בְּלֵב הָעָם, אֲשֶׁר אָהַב לְהִשְׁתַּעֲשֵׁעַ בְּסִפְרֵי חָכְמָתוֹ וּשְׁנִינוּתוֹ, הַמּוּבָאִים לִפְנֵיכֶם בְּסֵפֶר זֶה.

The inscription on Rabbi Yehonatans tombstone reflects on the great pain he experienced as a result of the persecution and insults he received during his lifetime. He offers advice that people should flee from positions of authority and the Rabbinate.

Here is buried Our Holy Rabbi
Rabbi of all of the diaspora
He headed the Yeshivah for fifty years
He had many students
He established protective boundaries for the Torah
He wrote many seforim
Our teacher Rabbi Yehonatan the memory
of the righteous should be a blessing
Head of the Rabbinical court of the three
communities AHU and the head of the Rabbinical
court of the holy community of Metz.
He died a painless death on Tuesday and he
was buried on the same day the 21st Elul.
'This is the Torah of someone who passes away in the tent.'[85]
The following was found in Reb Yehonatan's handwriting
[instructing] to be inscribed on his tombstone
All who pass by will see the engraved
lettering on the tombstone
The man that stood as a banner[86] *and*
was like a rose that blooms

---

85. This is a quotation of a Biblical verse that speaks of a person passing away. For the Hebrew words that translate to mean 'that dies in a tent,' each letter has a dot on top. This signifies that one should add up the numerical value of those letters and it will give you the Hebrew year of Reb Yehonatan's passing.

86. *Yeshayahu* 11:10

And returns to the dust[87] and his
appearance was like a ruined man
Please take to heart and return [to G-d]
with a victorious repentance
Pray plentifully for him to the G-d of the spirits
His soul should be gathered to Him,
and he should not be shunned
The merit of your actions should protect [him]
as the souls of the Jewish people are one
Teach your souls to despise honor and your
souls should flee from greatness
May his memory be a blessing.

In Hebrew, the first letter of each line[88]
spells the word Yehonatan.

The personality of the 'Wise Jew' crowned with the crown of Torah and the crown of Royalty reminds us of the wisdom and grace of the Jewish people. It remains engraved on the hearts of man who love to be entertained by his books of wisdom and learning that are brought in this book.

---

87. *Bereishit* 3:19

88. Many follow the custom that the inscription on the tombstone incorporates the name of the deceased with the first letter of each line spelling out the name.

GLOSSARY

Afikomen: On Pesach, as part of the seder, we eat the afikomen, the middle of the three matzot, which is broken in two. The larger part is put aside to be eaten at the end of the meal as the afikomen. In many families, it is custom for the young children to hide the afikomen and return it only after their father has promised to buy them a gift.

Aleinu: The last prayer of the morning service.

Arizal: Isaac ben Solomon Luria Ashkenazi (1534–1572) was a leading rabbi and Jewish mystic in the community of Safed in the Galilee. He is considered the father of contemporary Kabbalah, his teachings being referred to as Lurianic Kabbalah. He is sometimes known as the Ari in English.

av bet din: Head of the Jewish judicial court.

aveira: sin.

ba'al teshuvah: a Jew who has returned to Hashem and His Torah.

bar mitzvah: initiatory ceremony recognizing a boy as an adult.

bet din: Jewish court of law.

Bet Hamikdash: The Temple (There were two temples. The first built by King Solomon stood from 957 BCE–586 BCE, and the second built by Ezra and Nehemiya stood from 516 BCE–70 CE.)

bet midrash: house of study.

Berachot (aka Brachot): literal translation "blessing"; the first of the sixty-three tractates of the Talmud that comprise the oral tradition.

brit milah: circumcision ceremony.

chametz: leavened food product prohibited during the festival of Pesach.

cheder: elementary school.

chevra kaddisha: Jewish burial society.

Chumash: Torah.

daven/davening: pray/praying.

four species: Four plants mentioned in the Torah as being relevant to the festival of Sukkot—the *lulav*, *etrog*, myrtle and willow.

gabbai: sexton, custodian.

gaon: Torah giant.

hamantaschen: a three-cornered piece of dough with filling.

Haskalah movement: Often termed Jewish Enlightenment; literally "wisdom"; an intellectual movement among the Jews of Central and Eastern Europe. It arose as a defined ideological worldview during the 1770s, and its last stage ended around 1881.

Hanosi: the prince.

korban/korbanot: sacrifice(s).

Kodesh Hakodoshim: the Holy of Holies in the Temple.

maaseh: *tithe* (the one-tenth portion of produce given to charity).

Magen David: Star of David.

maggid: preacher.

Mah Tovu: the first prayer of the morning service.

Marcheshvan: eighth month of the Hebrew calendar.

Masechet/Masechtot: tractate(s); Talmudic literature that systematically examines a subject named for the main subject with which it deals.

mazel tov: a traditional greeting given to a person celebrating a happy occasion. It literally means "good energy."

Midrash: Is part of the oral tradition. It is a form of literature that interprets and elaborates upon biblical texts, mostly compiled from the fifth century CE through the medieval period. Books in this category generally share common methods of interpretation, like filling in gaps in stories. Sections of Midrash appear frequently throughout the Talmud. There are certain Midrashim that are very cryptic and are very challenging to comprehend. Such Midrashim are referred to as Midrash Plia (Wonderous Midrash).

mikvah: ritual pool of water

Minchah: afternoon prayer.

Minhagim: customs

minyan: quorum of ten Jewish men over the age of thirteen required to conduct shul services.

Mishloach Manot: gifts of food.

Mishnayot: The first major written collection of the oral Torah.

mussar: works pertaining to moral and ethical conduct.

negel vasser: literally means "water for the nails." It is the practice of washing one's hands in a specific manner using a two-handled cup and bowl prior to getting out of bed in the morning.

nekudot: dots or lines that indicate vowel sounds; tzerei are two adjoining dots; segal are three dots forming an upside-down triangle; and patach is a straight line.

oberrabbiner: chief rabbi.

posuk/posukim: verse(s).

pidyon haben: first-born redemption ceremony.

Purim: a day that commemorates the saving of the Jewish people from Haman, as recounted in the Book of Esther during the fourth century BCE.

Rabbeinu Hakodesh: our holy teacher

Rambam: Rabbi Moses ben Maimon (1135–1204) was a Talmudist, Halachist, physician, philosopher, and communal leader, known in the Jewish world by the acronym "Rambam" and to the world at large as "Maimonides." He is one of the most important figures in the history of Torah scholarship. The words "From Moses to Moses, none arose as Moses" are inscribed on his gravestone.

rosh yeshiva: head of an institution for advanced Talmudic study

seder: the meal on the first two nights of Pesach.

Sefer/seforim: holy book(s).

seudat hoda'ah: a festive meal thanking G-d for His kindness.

Shacharit: morning service.

shechita: the ritual slaughter of animals for meat.

Shemoneh Esrei: the central section of all Jewish prayer. It is recited while standing, in a very low voice that is audible only to the one praying. It is then repeated aloud by the person leading the service.

shidduch: an arranged marriage.

shiur: study session.

Shlomo Hamelech: King Solomon.

shochet/shochtim: ritual slaughterer(s).

Sholom aleichem: Traditional greeting when meeting someone.

siyum: the completion of any established unit of Torah study, such as the completion of a tractate of the Talmud.

tallit: prayer shawl.

talmid chochom/talmidei chachomim: Torah scholar(s)

Talmud: Text of the oral tradition; a record of the rabbinic debates in the second through fifth century on the teachings of the Torah.

Tanach: The 24 books that comprise the written tradition. The five books of Moses, the Prophets and the Writings.

tannaim: rabbinic sages whose rulings are recorded in the Mishnah.

tefillin: phylacteries worn during the morning service.

Tikkun Chatzot: midnight prayer.

tithe: the one-tenth portion of produce given to charity.

Tosafot: commentaries on the Talmud.

tzedakah: charity.

yetzer hara: evil inclination.

yetzer tov: positive inclination.

Yom Tov/Yomim Tovim: festival(s)

Yaarot Dvash

Moral exhortation of the true Torah giant Rabbi Yehonatan, my uncle[1], our master, our teacher, our leader that he addressed the public in the illustrious Metz community where he served as rabbi and spiritual leader. He occupied an exalted position. He disseminated Torah and taught many students who were very valued and became the giants of the generation. Happy are the people to whom this is so. Silence is the book's praise [as any praise given will never suffice]. This book does not need to be praised as it gives off a pleasant odor similar to persimmon oil. And in the Temple, everyone speaks of its glory.

Under the authority of the illustrious privileged Duke Karl Fredrich, Grand Duke of Baden[2].

May G-d elevate his stature and that of his wife and descendants. And may they be blessed with a pleasant and long life.

Printed here in the holy community of **Karlsruhe**

In the year[3] 'Listen my son to the exhortation of your father'[4]

---

1. The book was published by the author's nephew and disciple, R' Yehudah Leib, son of R' Moshe Wormish of Karlsruhe.

2. German noble (1728–1811).

3. The following verse has certain letters in a larger font. Adding the numerical value of these letters gives you the year the book was printed. The first part was printed in 1779 and the second in 1782.

4. שמע בני מוסר אביך

ספר

יערות דבש

היה תוכחת מוסר מה שדרש בדבי' אדמו' דודי הגאון אבי'תי מהו' יהונתן
זיל נקיק מי'ן המעוטרה : כשה' שם לרב וטורה : והי' יושב בישיבה של
מעלה : והרכ'ין שם תורה : והעמיד תלמידים הרבה : גאוני הדור וכלי
חמדה : אשרי העם שככה לו : ודומ' תהילה נאה לו : והכפר זה לא
צריך לפאריהו בשילולו : כי גיעגבו נתן ריח כשמן אפרסמק בכל פעלו :
ובהיכלו כבוד אומר כולו :

תחת ממשלת אדונינו הדוכס המיוחס המהולל

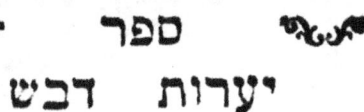

מארק גראאף צו באדין אונד הויך בעריג השם ירום הודו יתנשא אדינותיו לו
וגבירתו וגם לורעותיו ויאריך להם ישיהם ושנותיהם בטוב ובנעיסם אמן :

נדפס פה בקק

קארלסרוא

סלאת **שמע בני מוסר אניך** לפ'ק :

שַׁעַר הַסֵּפֶר "יַעֲרוֹת דְּבַשׁ" בִּדְפוּסוֹ הָרִאשׁוֹן

Acknowledgments

This is the third book I have written based on the teachings of Rabbi Yehonatan Eybeshitz, one of the greatest rabbis of the eighteenth century. Reb Yehonatan was as at home with the Talmud and Shulchan Aruch as he was in discussing philosophy and worldly affairs with kings, princes, and heads of the church.

In this endeavor, I am most fortunate to have been blessed with such wonderful partners as Richie and Julie Gerber. They relentlessly pursue their vision, and through the grace of Hashem, I am privileged to be part of it.

Julie is a direct descendant of Rabbi Yehonatan Eybeshitz. She and Richie are passionate about exploring their ancestor's life and learning his profound thoughts and ideas. All the stories in this book were originally written in Lashon Hakodesh Hebrew, making it in a sense a closed book for the English-speaking world. The Gerbers have tasked me with sharing these stories in English, thereby making them accessible to a far wider reading audience. The Gerbers are to be commended for their desire to share this treasure chest of knowledge and inspiration with the broad populace.

Our paths would never have crossed if it wasn't for the input of my dear son-in-law Rabbi Ephraim Duchman—a special *yesha koach* (thank you), Ephraim.

This book as the previous two has been greatly enhanced by the highly professional team The Book Couple: Carol Killman

Rosenberg, for her editing skills, and Gary Rosenberg, for the beautiful cover and layout. A great rabbi once said that Jewish books need to be aesthetically appealing and easy on the eye. Carol and Gary, you hit the bull's-eye.

I would like to dedicate this book to my wonderful children and grandchildren. They all continue to be a great source of nachas for myself and their late mother Rivkie in olam ha'emet. The greatest nachas Rivkie a"h and I have is seeing how they have established their own homes and the way they are raising their children in the manner they saw in their home and the homes of their grandparents.

I would also like to dedicate this in memory of my beloved family members who have passed away. While they are no longer present in this physical world, their memory and their shining example live on in their children, grandchildren, and great grandchildren.

My late wife, Rivkie, who passed away on the 19th of Adar 2 5774 (2014). Rivkie was a respected Rebbetzin and a devoted teacher. Her warmth and friendliness, humor and vibrancy, authenticity and compassion touched the lives of all who crossed her path.

My late father, Reb Meir Barber, who passed away on the 18th of Elul 5779 (2019). He was one of the pillars of the Sydney *frum* community. My father was a Holocaust survivor; he spent most of the war years with his family in Siberia. He was a child when the war broke out, never really having the opportunity of studying in a yeshivah. However, after the war, he ended up in Bergen-Belsen. He attended a yeshivah that had been established in what was once an infamous concentration camp. Prior to coming to Australia, his family received a bracha from a great tzaddik that he would have *dor yeshurum um'vorach* (Blessed offspring) who will continue in the righteous path of our tradition. May this blessing remain with his descendants for generations to come.

My father eventually made his way to Sydney, Australia, and in his small suitcase, he brought with him one of our family's great treasures. He brought his Gemorah with him. On the first page, it says his name and the name of the yeshivah, *Sheirit Hapleito* (The Surviving Remnant) Bergen-Belsen. Once a concentration camp, it had then become the home of Jewish learning and Jewish revival. Perhaps this encapsulates the secret of Jewish survival. The recognition of the inseparable bond between the Torah and the Jewish people. It speaks of the strength of the Jewish people that even in our darkest hours we continue to learn and teach Hashem's Torah. That Gemorah continues to inspire his children, grandchildren, and great grandchildren.

Only a few short months ago our family was given a treasure, one that we never knew existed. Buried in a box in someone's basement for over seventy years was another sefer my father must have brought with him on his journey to a country of refuge. Besides the obvious joy of discovering a sefer that my father had studied from way back in 1946, it was the name of the sefer that caused such joy and introspection. It was the *Shagaas Aryeh*.[5] The sefer is extremely challenging and is Torah study at a very high level. To imagine after living through *gehenom*(hell) in this world, my father enters a yeshiva that is studying Torah at the highest level. As a side note, the Shagaas Aryeh succeeded Reb Yehonatan as rabbi in Metz.

My late father-in-law Rabbi Asher Halevi Heber, who passed away on the 8th of Nisan 5780 (2020); he merited that the Lubavitcher Rebbe and Rebbetzin were the *kevaterin* at his bris in prewar Paris. For over forty years, he was a beloved teacher in Manhattan Jewish Day School. It was astounding to hear and read the accolades his students shared with the family at the time of his untimely passing. Many had been in his class

---

5. Reb Arye Leib (1695–1785), famed Talmudic scholar

more than thirty years before, and they were still able to recall so much of what he had taught them and how he had inspired them to lead Torah-observant lives coupled with a great thirst for the study of Torah.

My beloved uncle and aunt, Reb Shabsi and Rebecca Kornwasser; my uncle passed away on the 2nd of Adar 5772 (2012). He came from an illustrious family of Radomsk Chasidim. He was an everlasting link of the Chasidic world of prewar Poland and the Jewish world I grew up in in Australia. His stories of Chasidic life in Sosnowiec and his heroic self-sacrifice for Torah and mitzvos during the Holocaust inspire me to this very day.

Rebbeca Kornwasser passed away on the 21st of Shat 5779 (2019). Auntie Becca, as she was affectionately called, was beloved by everyone. She was imbued with great *simchat hachayim* (love of life), which she shared with all who knew her. One could say she lived to give. She had a heart of gold and only saw the good in people.

To my dear mother, Esther Barber, and my dear *shviger*, Nechama Heber. May you both find a level of solace in seeing the beautiful generations you are both the proud matriarchs of. May Hashem bless you both with many years of good health and be *zoche* to greet *Moshiach Tzidkeiynu b'karov mamosh*.

Rabbi Yacov Barber
19 Adar II 5784 (March 29, 2024)
marking the tenth yahrtzeit anniversary
of the passing of my dear wife

PUBLISHER'S ACKNOWLEDGMENTS

First and foremost, we would like to thank Rabbi Yacov Barber for writing this noteworthy book, *Gates of Wisdom*. Using his vast knowledge and scholarship, he has opened up gates long ago forgotten. Without him, this book would not exist. We truly cannot thank you enough.

We also extend our heartfelt gratitude to Rabbi Efraim Duchman, who connected us with his father-in-law, Rabbi Yacov Barber. Rabbi Duchman is the director of development at Colel Chabad and has helped us in myriad ways. We are honored to call Rabbi Duchman a friend.

Carol & Gary, The Book Couple, have done monumental work editing and designing this book. They have spent countless hours sharing their expertise and professionalism to create the book you now hold in your hands.

Many thanks to Rabbi Sruli Deutch of the Eastchester Chabad for sharing the story of Am Yisrael Chai with Julie on their way to the March for Israel in Washington, D.C., on November 14, 2023.

Words cannot express our sincerest gratitude to Eli Karagoulla O"bm and his wife, Patricia Bedoya. Eli was a member of our shul and was born in Israel. He generously worked on a first translation of *The Wise Jew* in order for us to understand what a pearl we had. Patricia worked with her late husband to make it more understandable to us. Many, many thanks!

Many thanks to our friend for life, Maine humorist, artist, musician, and television personality Tim Sample (TimSample. com) for creating the logo for Gerber's Miracle Publishers, which now graces several thought-provoking, wisdom-containing books.

SELECTED
REFERENCES

Harav Reb Yehonatan Eibshitz

Kivrei Tzadikim B'Ashkenaz

Sarai Hameah

Chad V'Cholok

HaChasidut

L'Binyamin Amar Shmot

Maleim Ziv

Sichos L'Noar

Mapik Margoliot

Binyan Shaul

About the Author

RABBI YACOV BARBER was born to Holocaust survivors. He is the father of six children and a proud grandfather. He has lived and studied in Israel, Canada, and Melbourne. He is currently living in New York. Having received both Rabbinic Ordination and Judiciary Ordination, he has also completed courses in palliative care, mediation, family violence, and arbitration.

Rabbi Barber is an internationally acclaimed motivational speaker and a much sought-after communicator on ethics as well as spiritual and personal growth. He has lectured across the United States, Europe, Australia, and Canada.

He is the author of *Generation to Generation: Insights into the Haggadah*; *Wit & Wisdom: Sermons on the Weekly Torah Reading*; *Pearls of Wisdom*, a translation of insights of Reb Yehonatan Eybeshitz on the weekly portion and the festivals; and *Sparks of Wisdom*, Reb Yehonatan Eybeshitz insights on a wide range of topics including modern-day applications.

For more information, visit RabbiBarber.com.